T0060084

THE EVERYTHING
LARGE-PRINT
WORD SEARCH BOOK
VOLUME 3

Dear Reader,

I go through several stages when solving a word search puzzle. At first glance, the letters appear to be random, but I know they're not. A few obvious words jump out, and then the searching begins. With a little concentration, a whole bunch of words are circled. The "aha" moments come quickly at this point, and it's hard to stop. The last few words usually drive me crazy; they're the ones that are diagonal and backward! Ultimately, I feel a nice sense of accomplishment when all the words are rounded up. The chaos of the grid has been overcome. Order rules!

If you love word search as much as I do, then I think you're going to enjoy this book. I've packed it full of puzzles that are easy on the eyes and fun for the brain. Each grid has a theme, and I cover a wide variety of interesting topics. I hope these puzzles are fun and relaxing for you!

Charles Timmerman

Welcome to the EVERYTHING® Series!

These handy, accessible books give you all you need to tackle a difficult project, gain a new hobby, comprehend a fascinating topic, prepare for an exam, or even brush up on something you learned back in school but have since forgotten.

You can choose to read an Everything® book from cover to cover or just pick out the information you want from our four useful boxes: e-questions, e-facts, e-alerts, and e-ssentials. We give you everything you need to know on the subject, but throw in a lot of fun stuff along the way, too.

We now have more than 400 Everything® books in print, spanning such wide-ranging categories as weddings, pregnancy, cooking, music instruction, foreign language, crafts, pets, New Age, and so much more. When you're done reading them all, you can finally say you know Everything®!

PUBLISHER Karen Cooper

DIRECTOR OF ACQUISITIONS AND INNOVATION Paula Munier

MANAGING EDITOR, EVERYTHING® SERIES Lisa Laing

COPY CHIEF Casey Ebert

ACQUISITIONS EDITOR Lisa Laing

EDITORIAL ASSISTANT Ross Weisman

EVERYTHING® SERIES COVER DESIGNER Erin Alexander

LAYOUT DESIGNERS Colleen Cunningham, Elisabeth Lariviere, Ashley Vierra, Denise Wallace

Visit the entire Everything® series at *www.everything.com*

THE
EVERYTHING®
LARGE-PRINT
WORD SEARCH
BOOK
VOLUME 3

150 quick, fun, easy-on-the-eyes puzzles

Charles Timmerman
Founder of Funster.com

Adams Media
New York London Toronto Sydney New Delhi

Adams Media
An Imprint of Simon & Schuster, Inc.
100 Technology Center Drive
Stoughton, MA 02072

Copyright © 2011 by Simon & Schuster, Inc.

All rights reserved, including the right to reproduce this book or portions thereof in any form whatsoever. For information address Adams Media Subsidiary Rights Department, 1230 Avenue of the Americas, New York, NY 10020.

An Everything® Series Book.
Everything® and everything.com® are registered trademarks of Simon & Schuster, Inc.

ADAMS MEDIA and colophon are trademarks of Simon and Schuster.

For information about special discounts for bulk purchases, please contact Simon & Schuster Special Sales at 1-866-506-1949 or business@simonandschuster.com.

The Simon & Schuster Speakers Bureau can bring authors to your live event. For more information or to book an event contact the Simon & Schuster Speakers Bureau at 1-866-248-3049 or visit our website at www.simonspeakers.com.

Manufactured in the United States of America

15 2024

ISBN 978-1-4405-2737-1

Many of the designations used by manufacturers and sellers to distinguish their products are claimed as trademarks. Where those designations appear in this book and Simon & Schuster, Inc., was aware of a trademark claim, the designations have been printed with initial capital letters.

Dedicated to
Suzanne, Calla, & Meryl

Acknowledgments

I would like to thank each and every one of the more than half a million people who have visited my website, *www.funster.com*, to play word games and puzzles. You have shown me how much fun puzzles can be and how addictive they can become!

It is a pleasure to acknowledge the folks at Adams Media who made this book possible. I particularly want to thank my editor, Lisa Laing, for so skillfully managing the many projects we have worked on together.

Contents

Introduction

The puzzles in this book are in the traditional word search format. Words in the list are hidden in the grid in any direction: up, down, forward, backward, or diagonally. The words are always found in a straight line, and letters are never skipped. Words can overlap. For example, the letters at the end of the word "MAST" could be used as the start of the word "STERN." Only the letters A to Z are used, and any spaces in an entry are removed. For example, "TROPICAL FISH" would be found in the grid as "TROPICALFISH." All punctuation marks, such as apostrophes and hyphens, are also omitted in the puzzles. Draw a circle around each word that you find in the grid. Then, cross the word off the list so that you will always know what words remain to be found.

A favorite strategy is to look for the first letter in a word, then see if the second letter is in any of the eight neighboring letters, and so on until the word is found. Or instead of searching for the first letter in a word, it is sometimes easier to look for letters that standout, like Q, U, X, and Z. Double letters in a word will also stand out and be easier to find in the grid. Another strategy is to simply scan each row, column, and diagonal, looking for any words.

Puzzles

ALTER

BACKSTITCH

BATTING

BINDING

BOBBIN

BUTTONHOLE

CLOTH

CUT

DARNING

DESIGN

EMBROIDERY

EYELET

FABRIC

GATHER

GUSSET

HEM

LINING

MACHINE

MATERIAL

NEEDLEWORK

PATCHWORK

PATTERN

PIN

PLEAT

POCKET

QUILTING

SCISSORS

SEAMSTRESS

SEWING

STITCHES

TACK

TAILOR

TECHNIQUES

THIMBLE

THREAD

TRIM

YARN

Sewing Circle

```
B X O P O C K E T E S S U G
K A L A I R E T A M Y T N N
H R C E L B M I H T E I I I
D T O K F A B R I C T T B N
A R O W S V R A H T P C B I
E Y E L E T O N A A H H O L
R J S T C L I B T E G E B G
H M R R L Q D T M L A S P N
T A O A U A E E C O T T L I
D C S E R R R P E H H A E W
E H S N N I Y A R N E C A E
S I I P A T C H W O R K T S
I N C I H C G N I T L I U Q
G E S N S E A M S T R E S S
N R O L I A T C Q U U I U U
C Q L G N I D N I B B C M A
```

Solution on Page 304

ALUMINUM	PROFILE
BANK	ROUND
BRASS	SAVE
BRONZE	SERIES
CHANGE	SHIELD
COINAGE	SMALL
COLLECTOR	SPEND
COPPER	STEEL
CURRENCY	TAILS
DATE	TREASURY
HEADS	USA
HISTORY	VALUE
INFLATION	WHEAT
JAR	YEAR
LIBERTY	ZINC
LINCOLN	
MEMORIAL	
METAL	
MINT	
MONEY	
ONE CENT	
PRESIDENT	

Penny

```
T J Z E Q Y B Q E U L A V Y
N P T M T S T L S A D S S Z
E Y R U S A E R T L M U B S
D M E N U B D E E I A R E L
I O L I C R M I N B O R Y I
S N H M O A H T M N I N A A
E E F U I S H N Z E L L U T
R Y U L N S F E S B L O Z A
P Q Y A A G M C A O A C Q E
J P R H G T R E N D M N R H
A R O R E A I N M I S I K W
R O T C E L L O C O Z L V G
X F S Y V P Y C N E R R U C
D I I J A S P E N D J I F I
C L H R S X R O U N D P A H
Q E G N A H C F C S T E E L
```

Solution on Page 304

PUZZLES • 5

AGED

ANIMAL

BARN

BUCKET

BUTTERMILK

CALCIUM

CASEIN

CATTLE

CHEESE

CHURN

COWS

CURDS

FACTORY

FARMERS

FOOD

GOATS

GRASS

HARVESTING

HEALTHY

HEIFER

ICE CREAM

INDUSTRY

LACTOSE

LOW FAT

MANURE

MILKING

PASTURE

POWDER

PROCESSING

PRODUCTS

SKIMMED

UDDER

WHEY

WHOLE

YOGURT

```
P P K W Y V U E U V F H X R
W O P M X O I F D D O O F E
H W M I L K I N G E C C O D
O D H E A L T H Y H G Q C D
L E I G N I T S E V R A H U
E R U N A M A E R C E C I C
F A R M E R S C Y E H W P H
G N I S S E C O R P G R A S
C L V F R T X A T C O W S W
A S A A E T M L S D H A T B
T T A M F U N A U E R U U A
T A N V I B M C D G I C R R
L O F C E N T T N N K N E N
E G L W H S A O I E L S B L
F A C T O R Y S T R U G O Y
C U R D S L D E M M I K S E
```

Solution on Page 304

ALBUM	PICTURE
ATHLETE	PLAYERS
BASEBALL	PRISTINE
BOXING	RACING
BUBBLE GUM	RARE
CARTOONS	ROOKIE
COLLECTOR	SCARCITY
COMIC BOOK	SELL
CONDITION	SETS
EBAY	SPORTS
FLEER	STATISTICS
FOIL	TELEVISION
FOOTBALL	TOPPS
GAMES	TRADING
GOLF	UPPER DECK
HOBBY	VALUABLE
HOCKEY	WRAPPER
IMAGE	
MINT	
PACK	
PAPERBOARD	
PERSON	

```
K D R F O I L E I K O O R S
C S C O N D I T I O N R C G
A T A O T E L E V I S I O N
P R T T R C S P P O T L R I
Y O H B A S E L L S F L A X
E P L A D P D L I K D A C O
K S E L I I R T L O G B I B
C C T L N C A M Y O U E N L
O A E E G T O U B B C S G A
H R L D S U B B B C A A W S
P C B A R R R L O I R B R R
E I A Z E E E A H M T M A E
R T U R E G P E D O O I P Y
S Y L B U E A P L C O N P A
O G A M E S P M U F N T E L
N Y V R A R E N I T S I R P
```

Solution on Page 304

ASSET	MONEY
BANKS	OPTIONS
BONDS	PENSION
BUSINESS	PERCENTAGE
CAPITAL	PRINCIPAL
COMMODITY	PROFIT
DEPOSIT	PROPERTY
DIVIDENDS	PURCHASE
DOW	RETURNS
ECONOMY	RISK
FINANCIAL	SAVINGS
FUNDS	SECURITY
FUTURES	SELL
GAINS	SILVER
GOLD	STOCK
INCOME	TIME
INTEREST	TRADE
LAND	VALUE
LOAN	
LOSS	
MARGIN	
MARKET	

Financial Investment

```
S N I A G K Q Z L S D N O B
S E I C P Q C A P I T A L S
G D L G E U P O V P I T F I
N A O L R I R I T L F T U L
I T S W C A D C A S O I T V
V Z S N E E M I H B R S U E
A D I Y N P C O U A P O R R
S R L D T N E S N F S P E E
P E S O A I I N T E R E S T
E B C N G N D I S I Y D K U
U L I U E R N O S I M Z N R
L F A S R C W K M A O E A N
A U S N O I T P O M N N B S
V N S M D Y T R E P O R P W
F D E D A R T Y P Q C C H B
Z S T T J K M A R K E T G S
```

Solution on Page 305

AIRWAVES

ANTENNA

AUDIENCE

BAND

BBC

BROADCAST

CABLE FM

CHANNEL

DIAL

FCC

FREQUENCY

INTERNET

LISTENER

MICROPHONE

MODULATION

MUSIC

NETWORKS

NPR

ON AIR

PROGRAM

PUBLIC

RADIO

RECEIVER

RECEPTION

SATELLITE

SHORTWAVE

SIGNAL

SIMULCAST

SIRIUS

STATIONS

TALK

TOWER

TRANSMIT

TUNER

Radio Broadcasting

```
I M R T R A N S M I T A L K
S R U A S T A T I O N S Q P
H E F S I M U L C A S T N Q
O N S R I N T E R N E T S B
R E I L E C A E O T D N A B
T T G R A Q V S P E P A T C
W S N R U I U H H N U U E N
A I A V E I D E O N R D L E
V L L C R F P I N A C I L T
E O E I D E T J E C Q E I W
S R S E V A W R I A Y N T O
R O U E L N O I T P E C E R
Q A N U Z V V R T O W E R K
A P D A M F E L B A C C F S
R O Y I I C H A N N E L I C
M A R G O R P U B L I C Z L
```

Solution on Page 305

BRAND

BROTH

CANS

CASSEROLE

CHICKEN

CHUNKY

CONDENSED

COOK

CRACKERS

CREAM

EAT

FOOD

HEALTHY

HOME

KIDS

KITCHEN

LABELS

MEAL

MMM GOOD

MUSHROOM

NOODLE

POP ART

PRODUCTS

RED

RICE

SALT

SODIUM

SOUP

STOCK

TOMATO

VARIETY

VEGETABLE

WARHOL

WHITE

Campbell's Soup

```
D B W V D M Y C U N H D H C
R S U V I K S Y Y R E D D R
M S O D N O O D L E I M M L
S A D U D V P R O D U C T S
H J H I P M E A L S X R E D
N C U K K L E G H D W E N H
E M A T L A S R E K C A R C
H N L S T D O S F T R M V O
C E E E S O N O U B A C N O
T K A J M E X H T O R B J K
I C F L D P R L L A B E L S
K I O N T D O O G M M M X E
K H O M E H J P L K C O T S
T C D Y R V Y T A E D E T I
D S N A C U C V A R I E T Y
I G W V X Z J W H I T E N Y
```

Solution on Page 305

PUZZLES • 15

ANATOMY

ANCIENT

ANIMALS

BIOLOGY

BIRDS

BONES

DATING

DINOSAURS

DISCOVERY

DNA

EARTH

ECOSYSTEM

EROSION

EVOLUTION

EXPERIMENT

EXTINCTION

FISH

FOSSILS

FUNGI

GEOLOGY

HUMAN

JURASSIC

LAB

LIFE

MESOZOIC

MUSEUM

OCEAN

ORGANISMS

PALEOZOIC

REPTILES

RESEARCH

ROCKS

SCIENTIST

SITE

STUDY

TAXONOMY

TRIASSIC

```
C B I O L O G Y D U T S A B
I M U S E U M S L A M I N A
O N O I S O R E S E A R C H
Z J F L T G P E N S D R I B
O U U A Q L H A P H N W E S
E R N B R T M N T T O S N S
L A G S R U A S O N I D T L
A S I A H G I T O E T L G I
P S E N N T R I C M U S E S
C I E I N I T O E I L K O S
A C T E A C S F A R O C L O
N A I S N Y I M N E V O O F
D C S I S L Y Y S P E R G I
S I T T Y M O N O X A T Y S
C X E D I S C O V E R Y T H
E M E S O Z O I C S E N O B
```

Solution on Page 305

BAR

BEAN BAG

BEDROOM

BENCHES

BOOKCASE

CABINET

COFFEE TABLE

COUCH

CREDENZA

CUPBOARDS

DAVENPORT

DRAWERS

DRAWING BOARD

DRESSERS

END TABLE

FOOTSTOOL

HEADBOARD

HOPE CHEST

HUTCH

LIVING ROOM

LOVE SEAT

METAL

NIGHTSTAND

OTTOMAN

PLASTIC

RECLINER

SEATING

SIDEBOARD

SOFA

TABLES

WARDROBE

WICKER

WOODEN

Furniture Types

```
B T N W Y F O M F L A T E M
E E A S D R A O B P U C G O
N N M Q A W O O D E N D T O
C I O B H T O R S A R A P R
H B T U S K A G Z A E L E D
E A T T C O S N W S A K T E
S C O A B R E I E S C R S B
H O S D E D N V T I S E E O
L E A W E G O I W B E N H R
F E A R B L C L Z E L I C D
H R C O F F E E T A B L E R
D N A T S T H G I N A C P A
T R O P N E V A D B T E O W
D R E S S E R S K A D R H W
A F O S E A T I N G N J E N
C O U C H D R A O B E D I S
```

Solution on Page 306

ARCHITECT

BIDDING

BRICK

BUILDINGS

BULLDOZER

CARPENTER

CONTRACTOR

CRANES

DELAYS

DESIGN

ENGINEER

EQUIPMENT

ERECT

EXECUTION

FOUNDATION

FRAME

HOUSES

JOB

LABORER

LAND

LOGISTICS

MANAGER

MATERIALS

PLANNING

PROJECT

PROPERTY

SAFETY

SITE

SKYSCRAPER

STEEL

STONE

STRUCTURE

TRADE

WOOD

WORKERS

Construction

```
C A R P E N T E R S U N C G
F R A M E P S P R G S G N E
S C W M S R K K E N E I E R
R H O V C O Y C E I D S M E
E I O N I P S I N D A E A G
K T D A T E C R I L R D T A
R E T N S R R B G I T J E N
O C N O I T A D N U O F R A
W T E I G Y P C E B C E I M
H C M T O T E L T R Z R A S
O E P U L E R D A O I E L Y
U J I C B F N N D N R C S A
S O U E K A E L S L N T T L
E R Q X L S L E E T S I O E
S P E E R U T C U R T S N D
W Z L A B O R E R S I T E G
```

Solution on Page 306

ADDRESS	INTERNET
BLOG	LINKS
BROWSER	NETWORK
BUSINESS	NEWS
CLICK	ONLINE
COMPUTER	PLAIN TEXT
CONTENT	SEARCH
DESIGN	SERVER
DOCUMENT	SITE
DOMAIN	SOCIAL
EBAY	URL
EMAIL	VIDEOS
FACEBOOK	VISIT
FORUM	WEB PAGES
GAMES	WWW
GOOGLE	
HOMEPAGE	
HOST	
HTML	
HTTP	
HYPERLINK	
IMAGES	

```
W D G U B R T H F Z X N Q E
D E Z O L Y H E T P E Z G Y
H T M C O N T E N T X A A V
S E M A G G M N W R P B U I
M S O C I A L O I E E L Y S
U S K N I L R E M A R T R I
R E K S M K D O C U M E N T
O G N S G S H S P L T O F I
F A C E B O O K S U I U D O
H M K N I L R E P Y H C N Q
C I R I U D G M D S K L K D
R D E S A A O H S I I W E P
A K V U P C A O W N V S W S
E F R B R O W S E R I W I G
S S E R D D A T N G W T G Y
J W S S P L A I N T E X T E
```

Solution on Page 306

AMERICA	SELL
BUSINESS	SERVICES
BUYING	SHOPPING
CAPITALIST	SOCIETY
CONSUMER	SPEND
COST	STATUS
CREDIT	STORE
DEMAND	SUPPLY
DESIRE	TRADE
ECONOMY	WANT
GOODS	WASTE
INDUSTRY	WEALTH
MALL	
MARKETING	
MONEY	
PACKAGING	
PEOPLE	
PRODUCTS	
PROFIT	
PURCHASING	
RETAIL	
RIGHTS	

Consumerism

```
Y M J G N I S A H C R U P G
P L Z R P A C K A G I N G X
Z B P S H O P P I N G T P G
T U J P G N I Y U B D Q A O
S S Y K U T U N N Z D Q U O
G I T W A S T E D E M A N D
H N E L D N E P S U T A T S
R E I S E R V I C E S Y U E
E S C T L J R L C I M T P L
T S O S E E A T O O Z P R L
A J S X C K M O N E Y R O Y
I S T H G I R O S A W O D R
L T Z W V T C A U N W F U M
P E O P L E V A M E R I C A
H T L A E W C R E D I T T L
C O S T R A D E R O T S S L
```

Solution on Page 306

ATOMS	PHENOMENA
CALCULUS	PHYSICAL
CONCEPTS	QUANTUM
EINSTEIN	QUARKS
ELECTRON	RELATIVITY
ENERGY	RESEARCH
EXPERIMENT	SCIENTIST
FORMULA	SPEED
GAS	STUDY
GRAVITY	TECHNOLOGY
LAWS	THEORY
LIGHT	UNIVERSE
MAGNETISM	VELOCITY
MASS	
MATTER	
MECHANICS	
MOMENTUM	
MOTION	
NATURE	
NEWTON	
NUCLEAR	
PARTICLES	

```
E S R E V I N U C L E A R W
M U D C X T H E O R Y M D R
A L I G H T Y T I C O L E V
S U X P A R T I C L E S E S
S C I E N T I S T U D Y P K
N L P Y T I V A R G A S S R
O A H G S C I N A H C E M A
T C E M A T T E R U T A N U
W I N H C R A E S E R K S Q
E S O Y G O L O N H C E T U
N Y M S I T E N G A M I P A
E H E X P E R I M E N T E N
R P N I E T S N I E S R C T
G L A W S E L E C T R O N U
Y N O I T O M U T N E M O M
S M O T A F O R M U L A C E
```

Solution on Page 307

AUTOMATION	MICROWAVE
BLENDER	MIXER
CAMCORDER	OVENS
CAMERAS	RANGE
CLEANING	REPAIR
CLOCKS	SERVICE
COMPACTOR	SMALL
COOKING	STOVE
DEVICES	TECHNOLOGY
DISHWASHER	TELEPHONE
DOMESTIC	TOASTER
DRYER	WASHING
ELECTRICAL	
FREEZER	
HEATER	
HOUSEHOLD	
IRON	
KITCHEN	
LOAD	
MACHINES	
MAJOR	
MECHANICAL	

Home Appliance

```
S D A O L A C I N A H C E M
S K C O L C S T O V E N S G
G N I N A E L C I H D Y Y N
N N E H C T I K T R L G R I
I R E X I M U M A J O R E K
H F X R R S N M L H U T O
S R B E T E G Z O L E E A O
A E M T C E H N T A S C E C
W E I S E A H S U M U I H I
R Z C A L C M S A S O V D T
E E R O E J K C E W H R N S
P R O T C A P M O C H E O E
A N W B L E N D E R I S R M
I S A R E M A C F P D V I O
R Q V T E L E P H O N E E D
X S E N I H C A M R E Y R D
```

Solution on Page 307

ALL TRADES

BUILD

CALL

CARPENTRY

CONSTRUCT

CONTRACTOR

DRILL

DRYWALL

ELECTRICAL

EXTERIOR

FIXING

FLOOR

HAMMER

HANDY

HELPFUL

HOME

HOUSEHOLD

INTERIOR

LEAKS

LICENSED

LIGHT BULB

NAILS

NEIGHBOR

ODD JOBS

PAINTING

PIPES

PLUMBING

PROJECTS

REMODELING

REPAIRS

SERVICE

SKILLED

USEFUL

VAN

WOOD

WORK

```
C Y D N A H I N T E R I O R
A X P O P R O J E C T S O E R
R N L I O A S G N I X I F P
P E U D P W I B R A R U O A
E I M L A E L N O E I Z O I
N G B O E L S I T J M L C R
T H I H D L L X C I D O S S
R B N E R E E T A E N D H B
Y O G S Y Z L C R S N G O U
R R R U W P H I T A K S R I
E U O O A E Z R N R D A E L
M S O H L L U A O G I E E D
M E L P L C V W C G F C S L
A F F A T E C I V R E S A W
H U C F H B L U B T H G I L
L L I R D E L L I K S O T W
```

Solution on Page 307

BIRTH

BOND

BROTHER

CHILDHOOD

CHILDREN

CLOSE

ETYMOLOGY

FAMILY

FATHER

FIGHTING

FOSTER

FRIEND

FULL

GENETICS

GIRL

HALF

HOME

JEALOUSY

KINSHIP

LOVE

MIDDLE

MOTHER

OLDER

PARENTS

RELATIVE

RIVALRY

SHARE

SISTER

STEP

TOGETHER

TWINS

YOUNGEST

```
A N P A R Y S U O L A E J I
E T I N M U Z C L O S E K Q
R M O F R J G P I H S N I K
A Z O L Q C R E H T O M H E
H V U H F R I E N D E G K R
S N I W T P J V O X I N R T
T I X Y G O L O M Y T E E O
N S G I A B H L F S L R H G
E U N M I D D L E A L D T E
R G I R L X A G T B S L A T
A E T I F H N I Y O I I F H
P H H J K U V J L N S H S E
N C G T O E L D I D T C A R
O U I Y O U E L M P E T S A
N E F A U R I V A L R Y D H
U F P T G A B K F O S T E R
```

Solution on Page 307

ART	PATTERNS
BATHROOM	PLASTIC
CEILING	PORCELAIN
CEMENT	QUARRY
CERAMIC	ROOFS
COLOR	SAW
DECORATIVE	SHOWERS
DESIGNER	SLATE
FLAT	SQUARE
FLOORING	WALLS
GLAZED	WATER
GLUE	WHITE
GRANITE	WOOD
GROUT	
HARD	
KITCHEN	
LAY	
LIMESTONE	
MARBLE	
METAL	
MORTAR	
MOSAICS	

```
W I M O R T A R O L O C A Y
K R O O F S E G F L A T W H
U L K O S S R E W O H S E A
Q O D Q U A R R Y W A T E R
K G R E N G I S E D A T F D
J I U I C D G C S L I C G M
B A T H R O O M S H H E L Q
S E N C P F R O W A N R A P
Q C T I H L P A W O W A Z S
U G T R A E A A T N E M E C
A M E T A L N S T I L I D R
R G N I L I E C T T V C J X
E L B R A M J C F I E E F Z
J U L F I T U O R G C R O T
W A L L S C F L O O R I N G
Y N F G S L J C N F P B Y S
```

Solution on Page 308

ACTIVITY	POLITICS
AEROBATICS	RECREATION
AMATEUR	RUGBY
ARCHERY	RULES
ATHLETIC	RUNNING
BASEBALL	SCORE
BASKETBALL	SOFTBALL
BOWLING	SWIMMING
BOXING	TEAM SPORT
CRICKET	TENNIS
CURLING	TRAINING
EQUIPMENT	
ETHICS	
FOOTBALL	
GAME	
GOLF	
GYMNASTICS	
LACROSSE	
MEDICINE	
NUTRITION	
PHYSICAL	
PLAYERS	

Sporting Chance

```
A T H L E T I C U R L I N G
S C O R E Q S O F T B A L L
R A M A T E U R U N N I N G
E Z Y N O I T I R T U N O G
Y B G U R B N G P E M A G N
A L N Y T R O P S M A E T I
L T I T M L I Y L P E G L L
P E N E F N T L L O T N H W
H K I N E I A M A L H I T O
Y C A N V B E S B I I M Y B
S I R I E D R X T T C M R O
I R T S I R C V E I S I E X
C C A C U V E X K C C W H I
A B I L A C R O S S E S C N
L N E F O O T B A L L L R G
E S N S C I T A B O R E A T
```

Solution on Page 308

ALUMINUM	SAUCEPANS
BOWLS	SILICONE
BUNDT PAN	SKILLET
CAKE PAN	STOCK POT
CASSEROLE	STONEWARE
CAST IRON	TEFLON
CERAMIC	UTENSILS
COPPER	WOK
DUTCH OVEN	
FOOD	
FRYING PAN	
GLASS	
GRIDDLES	
KITCHEN	
LADLE	
LOAF PAN	
METAL	
NONSTICK	
PIE PAN	
POTS	
PYREX	
ROASTING	

Cookware

```
L K C I T S N O N Q R Z S A
A A F E N O C I L I S S L Q
T P D P I E P A N C A U I C
E P C L X R O K H U M X S I
M C A K E P A N C I Q S N M
J V S E R A W E N O T S E A
Z N S Q Y X P U A O T Q T R
Y A E C P A M E P S E S U E
H P R V N Z K B F S F E B C
T G O S O O I U A A L L B O
T N L K R H T N O L O D O P
W I E I I R C D L G N D W P
K Y F L T F H T O B W I L E
A R R L S M E P U O M R S R
T F K E A F N A K D F G D T
P P S T C K G N I T S A O R
```

Solution on Page 308

ANALYSIS	NAMES
ANCESTRY	PARENTS
BAPTISM	PAST
BIRTH	PEDIGREES
BLOODLINE	PEOPLE
BORN	RECORDS
BROTHER	RELATIVES
CENSUS	RESEARCH
CHILDREN	SIBLINGS
COUSIN	SOCIETY
DATA	SOFTWARE
DNA	SURNAME
FAMILIES	TRADITIONS
FATHER	TREE
HERALDRY	
HISTORICAL	
KINSHIP	
LIBRARY	
LINEAGES	
LOCATION	
MARRIAGES	
MOTHER	

```
S E G A E N I L D O O L B P
U U T P K S O F T W A R E R
P A S T N O I T A C O L T E
D D N N R O B E I M B F Y L
H C R A E S E R E A R A R A
B Y T E I C O S N R O M D T
A S N O I T I D A R T I L I
P Y R T S E C N A I H L A V
T R S I S Y L A N A E I R E
I A H F J P E D I G R E E S
S R N C H I L D R E N S H T
M B S G N I L B I S E M A N
N I S U O C P S U R N A M E
E L P O E P P S D R O C E R
K X R E H T A F B I R T H A
M O T H E R K I N S H I P P
```

Solution on Page 308

ACTIVIST

ACTRESS

AWARDS

BLACK

BROADWAY

CELEBRITY

COMEDIENNE

EMMY AWARD

FEMALE

FILM

GHOST

GRAMMY

GUINAN

LION KING

MOTHER

MOVIES

NUN

OSCAR

PRODUCER

SINGER

SISTER ACT

SOAPDISH

SONGWRITER

STAND UP

STAR TREK

SUCCESSFUL

TALENTED

TELEVISION

THE VIEW

TONY

VOICE

Whoopi Goldberg

```
T A L E N T E D S I N G E R
D B S M S O N G W R I T E R
C R T N O S N B Y M M A R G
T O A C N V E T H E V I E W
D S K W A F I L M L S S L B
P N I I A R D E V I U L L G
D U I V B Y E U S O C A V H
D N D E I T M T W N C N K O
R I L N Y T O M S K E F E S
A E A M A V C N E I S E R T
C M W I W T W A Y N S M T V
S O A P D I S H G G F A R O
O T R N A N I U G A U L A I
G H D N O I S I V E L E T C
S E S J R E C U D O R P S E
O R I Q B S A C T R E S S N
```

Solution on Page 309

ALLOY

ASSAY

BASE METAL

BRASS

BRONZE

BULLION

CAMEO

CARAT

CENT

CIRCULATED

COINS

COLLECTION

CONDITION

COPPER

CURRENCY

DATE

DESIGN

DIME

EAGLE

ENGRAVER

ERROR

EURO

FACE VALUE

GOLD

GRADING

LUSTER

MEDALLIONS

MINT

MONEY

MOTTO

NICKEL

OBVERSE

PATINA

PAYMENT

PROOF

QUARTER

RARE

SILVER

TOKENS

TRADE

Numismatics

```
F R A L A T E M E S A B G S
R E T R A U Q D E S I G N C
E V N O I T I D N O C O U L
V C O P P E R A R O I R E Y
L A I R E T S U L L R K E E
I M L E M F E L L E C E L N
S E L T I A E A N I U S G O
D O U A N C D C N G L R A M
B J B D T E Y E O P A E E O
R R N I M V M L M D T V R T
A S O I T A D Y I E E B R T
S N D N S L C N A T D O O O
S E I N Z U G A I P N A R Z
A K I T R E V A R G N E R B
Y O W Z A L L O Y A X K C T
C T S H E P R O O F T W W I
```

Solution on Page 309

ARTICLES

AUDIENCE

BLOG

BROADCAST

COLUMNIST

COPY

EDITING

EDITORS

EVENTS

FACTS

INFORM

INTERVIEW

ISSUES

JOURNALIST

LEAD

MAGAZINE

MASS MEDIA

NEWSPAPERS

ONLINE

OPINION

PRESS

PRINT

RADIO

REPORTING

RESEARCH

SCHOOL

SOURCE

STORY

TELEVISION

TRENDS

TRUTH

WAR

WRITING

Journalism

```
P S O U R C E D I T I N G Z
R T R E N D S A S R I D N C
E V E N T S I I A N A W I L
S N D L C E L D T E N D T B
S C I H E A C E L E F K I L
M T O Z N V R M W C A Q R O
V O O R A V I S P I C H W G
L G U R I G P S R N T A D E
B O N E Y A A A I F S U U X
J S W I P P R M N O I D E I
Q E Z E T A O T T R N I D M
H U R M W R B C I M M E I T
T S A C D A O R B C U N T G
U S N O I N I P O N L C O R
R I O O N L I N E H O E R Y
T W H M R E S E A R C H S V
```

Solution on Page 309

ANATOMY	NUCLEUS
ANIMALS	ORGANISMS
BACTERIA	PHYSIOLOGY
BOTANY	PROTEIN
CELLULAR	RESEARCH
CHEMISTRY	SCIENCE
CLASS	SPECIES
DARWIN	STRUCTURE
DNA	STUDY
ECOLOGY	TAXONOMY
EVOLUTION	TISSUES
FUNCTION	
GENETICS	
GROWTH	
HEREDITY	
HUMAN	
KINGDOM	
LABORATORY	
LIFE	
MEDICINE	
MICROSCOPE	
MOLECULES	

```
C E L L U L A R D A R W I N
A N D A H G N I E T O R P A
Z I S Z B N O I T C N U F M
S C E Y G O L O I S Y H P U
P I U T I I R E S E A R C H
E D S I E T B A N I M A L S
C E S D E U A N T L I F E A
I M I E R L C A S O C L C O
E O T R U O T T U H R P N R
S D A E T V E O E Y O Y E G
Y G X H C E R M L G S D I A
N N O T U U I Y C O C U C N
A I N W R S A L U L O T S I
T K O O T N A N N O P S M S
O G M R S S E L U C E L O M
B F Y G S K G E N E T I C S
```

Solution on Page 309

ANCESTOR	MAMMOTH
ANIMALS	ORGANISM
BIOLOGY	PAST
CARE	PLANTS
CHANGE	POLLUTION
DEATH	PRESERVE
DINOSAURS	RAIN FOREST
DISAPPEAR	RARE
DISEASE	SCIENCE
DODO	SPECIES
ECOLOGY	STUDY
ENDANGERED	SURVIVE
EVOLUTION	THREATENED
FOSSILS	
GENE POOL	
GENETICS	
GONE	
HABITAT	
HISTORY	
HUMAN	
HUNTING	
LOST	

```
P A S T S R U A S O N I D N
A N E H A B I T A T E E O A
M O C S D E A T H R R E D M
B I O L O G Y R A E A S O U
P T L E N M E R G I C A U H
L U O V R A I N F O R E S T
A L G R T R A E P P A S I D
N O Y E Y D U T S O L I M H
T V N S N N U G R L S D S U
S E G E N E P O O L L C I N
D S U R V I V E T U I H N T
L X S P E C I E S T S A A I
V H I S T O R Y E I S N G N
H T O M M A M N C O O G R G
S C I E N C E V N N F E O Y
K D E N O G S L A M I N A B
```

Solution on Page 310

ALUMINUM

BATTERIES

BINS

BOTTLES

CANS

CARDBOARD

CENTER

COLLECTION

COMPOST

CONSUMER

CONTAINER

EARTH

ECOLOGY

ENERGY

GARBAGE

GLASS

GREEN

LANDFILL

MATERIALS

METALS

MONEY

NEWSPAPER

PACKAGING

PLANET

PLASTICS

POLLUTION

RECYCLE

REDUCE

RENEW

RESOURCES

REUSE

SALVAGE

SAVING

SORTING

STEEL

TEXTILES

TRASH

```
R M S A V I N G P V S N I B
E R E M U S N O C A N S O G
U C D T S E L I T X E T N N
S C O S A L V A G E T I E Y
E O N L U L P S I L T E G V
R M Y T L L S H E R R R N X
L P I G A E S S O G E S I A
A O R N O A C S S N N T G L
N S E E R L E T E F I E A U
D T S T T G O W I M A E K M
F H O A A N S C R O T L C I
I T U B L P E E E N N C A N
L R R X A G D C T E O Y P U
L A C P Q U Z U T Y C C I M
G E E S C I T S A L P E R T
R R S E C A R D B O A R D S
```

Solution on Page 310

ACTOR

ALBUM

ARMY

ARTIST

BLUE SUEDE

COLONEL

CONCERT

COUNTRY

DANCE

FAMOUS

GOSPEL

GRACELAND

GRAMMYS

GUITAR

HAIR

HAWAII

HIPS

HOUND DOG

ICON

IDOL

JUMPSUIT

LAS VEGAS

LEATHER

LISA MARIE

MEMPHIS

MOVIES

MUSICIAN

PERFORMER

POPULAR

PRISCILLA

RECORDS

ROCK

SIDEBURNS

SINGER

SONGS

STAR

TENNESSEE

THE KING

TOUR

TUPELO

```
G Y N O C I J P G U I T A R
S M M Y R T N U O C R I L C
Y R E C O R D S M P N D B O
M A M B A C T O R P U O U N
M P P L A S V E G A S L M C
A E H U H I P S G A T U A E
R R I E E K C O R R C S I R
G F S S I B I R A T O O N T
O O I U P R I S C I L L A H
S R D E O A A K E S O E I E
P M E D H M W M L T N P C K
E E B E N K A W A D E U I I
L R U O T U H F N S L T S N
M L R S G N O S D N I T U G
S I N G E R E H T A E L M B
E E S S E N N E T D A N C E
```

Solution on Page 310

AMATEUR	JOCKEY
AMBLE	JUMPING
ARABIAN	MANE
ARENA	MARE
BOLTING	PONY
BRIDLE	POSTING
BUCKING	RACE
CANTER	REINS
COAT	RIDING
COLT	RODEO
CROP	SADDLE
ENGLISH	STALLION
EQUINE	STIRRUPS
FILLY	STRIDE
FOAL	TACK
FURLONG	TROT
GAIT	WESTERN
GALLOP	WHINNY
GELDING	
HALTER	
HARNESS	
HOOF	

```
A Y D S M X Z W R O D E O G
E N A M K X H O Y E K C O J
E G E G R I D I N G I A G R
B R H R N W E S T E R N K R
R F A N A B A G E L X T S T
I I Y M G O M A N D R E O F
D L B P N L A S I I E R O N
L L T E O T T T U N T A K Y
E Y I D L I E A Q G L S P N
N J Q I R N U L E N A A O O
G U H R U G R L A I H D L P
L M U T F Y J I X K H D L K
I P P S L C B O O C O L A C
S I N O O A E N W U O E G A
H N H A R N E S S B F L J T
G G T A E C A R J G A I T Y
```

Solution on Page 310

BACKYARD

BARN

BIKES

BUILDING

DOORS

EQUIPMENT

FARM

GARAGE

GARDENING

HOBBIES

HOOKS

HOUSE

KEEP

LAWN MOWER

LOCKED

METAL

OUTSIDE

PAINT

PLASTIC

POTTING

ROOF

SHELTER

SHELVES

SMALL

SPACE

STEEL

STORAGE

STRUCTURE

SUPPLIES

TOOLS

VINYL

WALLS

WOODEN

WORKSHOP

```
X W G M S T O R A G E L O P
S P A C E S R F A N X L L N
E P A I N T B R N I V A O Y
D R A Y K C A B G T S M C S
I E E L Q G R L N T N S K L
S T R W E G N U I O M S E L
T L U O O E N C N P H E D A
U E T R M M T I E O O I K W
O H C K J R N S D U B L H T
Y S U S E A E W R L B P U O
M K R H S F M O A V I P K O
T O T O U Y P O G L E U I L
E O S P O I I D K C S S B S
G H C E H D U E V I N Y L P
L J P E P H Q N F O O R T E
B B I K E S E V L E H S L M
```

Solution on Page 311

ANALYZE

BIOLOGY

CHEMISTRY

CONCLUSION

CONTROL

DATA

EMPIRICAL

EXPERIMENT

HYPOTHESIS

INQUIRY

KNOWLEDGE

LAB

LOGIC

MEASURABLE

METHOD

MODEL

OBJECTIVE

OBSERVE

PHENOMENA

PREDICTION

PROCEDURE

QUESTION

REACTION

REASONING

RESEARCH

RESULTS

RETEST

SCIENTISTS

STEPS

TECHNIQUES

THEORIES

```
S T L U S E R E S E A R C H
E V I T C E J B O P T U H T
G N I N O S A E R H A S E I
D P R O C E D U R E D C M N
E M P I R I C A L N N I I Q
L O R T N O C R S O M E S U
W S E E X P E R I M E N T I
O E D J R T Q S S E A T R R
N U I L E L U L E N S I Y Y
K Q C S A L E A H A U S G E
D I T B C O S N T L R T O V
O N I N T G T A O E A S L R
H H O W I I I L P D B T O E
T C N P O C O Y Y O L E I S
E E B S N X N Z H M E P B B
M T H E O R I E S J F S Y O
```

Solution on Page 311

AGING

BABY OIL

BEAUTY

BIKINI

BOOTHS

BRONZER

COLOR

COPPERTONE

DARK

EXPOSURE

FRECKLES

HEALTH

HOT

LOTION

PALE

PROTECT

RELAXING

RESORT

SALON

SPF

SUMMER

SUNBATHING

SUNBURN

SUNGLASSES

SUNLIGHT

SUNSCREEN

SWIMMING

UV RAYS

VITAMIN D

WRINKLE

Get Some Sun

```
C G N I M M I W S A L O N H
O G N P T A H T B O O T H S
P O V I T A M I N D T C U T
P H K K H E A L T H L E V B
E S H N O T O Y G S E T R I
R K R E T M A I T S S O A K
T T O E G K L B T U N R Y I
O R L R B N A O N Z A P S N
N E O C U G B G E U R E B I
E M C S I O L R X Q S R B P
L M U N E A R I P A L E K W
K U G U S R A N O I T O L P
N S I S P F J S S Y C K L K
I N E N R U B N U S B W R F
R S S E L K C E R F Q A U P
W L G N I X A L E R D R B S
```

Solution on Page 311

BAKING

BISCUIT

BROWNIES

BUTTER

CHEF

CHIPS

CHOCOLATE

CUTTER

DESSERT

DOUGH

DROP

EGGS

FAT

FLAT

FLOUR

FRUITS

GINGER

GIRL SCOUT

ICING

JAR

MILK

MONSTER

NUTS

OATMEAL

OREO

OVEN

PRESSED

RAISIN

RECIPE

ROUND

SHORTBREAD

SNACK

SOFT

SPICES

SUGAR

SWEET

TREAT

VANILLA

Cookies

```
R H G U O D N U O R L F E Y
U E K E G I R L S C O U T Q
O K C H I P S C H E F H S X
L C W I C H O C O L A T E L
F R U T P E E P R J E I I Z
Q B U T T E R B T Y G U N N
S W E E T E O R B N G C W X
O P M X S E E V R H S S O U
F O F S A S R J E T P I R S
R R E T S N O M A N I B B U
C D A E R S A F D R C A S G
A L D E T I T F O S E K N A
F K M L C R M I N I S I A R
Q T G I N G E R U T J N C H
V A N I L L A A U R L G K O
B G T H H K L N T C F B X A
```

Solution on Page 311

ALGORITHMS	NUMBER
BASIC	OBJECT
COBOL	PASCAL
CODE	PERL
COMMANDS	PROGRAMS
COMPILER	PYTHON
COMPUTERS	RUBY
DATA	SCIENCE
DEBUG	SEMANTICS
DESIGN	SOFTWARE
ENGINEER	SQL
EXECUTE	SYMBOLS
EXPRESSION	SYNTAX
FORTRAN	TECHNOLOGY
FUNCTIONAL	TYPE
HTML	
INPUT	
JAVASCRIPT	
LINES	
LOGIC	
MACHINE	
MICROSOFT	

Programming Languages

```
O T L N G I S E D O C T T C
B Y P R E E N I G N E F S N
J P A V E I N F C C O B O L
E E S U H P O O H S A H F Y
C H C C U R M N O S T C T H
T T A T T M O R M Y A O W C
P M L R A L C H P I D M A I
I L A N O I T C N U F P R S
R N D G M I G U B E D U E A
C S Y P R O G R A M S T T B
S A N O I S S E R P X E U R
A Q G B C O M P I L E R C U
V L L S E M A N T I C S E B
A S Y M B O L S E N I L X Y
J X A T N Y S C I E N C E I
L O G I C W D N U M B E R G
```

Solution on Page 312

AYURVEDA

BODY WORK

CHINESE

CURE

DIET

DISEASE

DOCTOR

ENERGY

FASTING

HEALING

HERBALISM

HERBOLOGY

HOLISTIC

HOMEOPATHY

HYPNOSIS

LIFESTYLE

MASSAGE

MEDITATION

MIND

NATUROPATH

OSTEOPATHY

PLANTS

REIKI

REMEDIES

SHIATSU

SPIRITUAL

SUPPLEMENT

TEA

THERAPY

TREATMENT

VEGAN

WATER

WELLNESS

YOGA

68

Alternative Medicine

```
O G L Y P A R E H T E I D R
R Y C A H E R B A L I S M O
D G G H U T N E M T A E R T
S R N O I T A T I D E M G C
S E I A L N I P K K Y H N O
E N T R G O E R O N I T I D
N E S E N E B S I E E A L F
L C A M T W V R E P M P A K
L I F E S T Y L E T S O E R
E T A D U S T A I H S R H O
W S D I S E A S E E R U C W
A I N E O S T E O P A T H Y
T L I S A D E V R U Y A R D
E O M S U P P L E M E N T O
R H Y P N O S I S Y O G A B
V M A S S A G E P L A N T S
```

Solution on Page 312

PUZZLES • **69**

ABSINTHE

ALCOHOL

BARLEY

BEER

BOOZE

BOTTLE

BOURBON

BRANDY

CHAMPAGNE

COGNAC

DRINKING

ETHANOL

GIN

GLASS

HOPS

LAGER

LIQUOR

MEAD

MIXED

PARTY

PORT

PROOF

PUB

RUM

SCHNAPPS

SCOTCH

SHERRY

SHOTS

SPIRITS

TEQUILA

VERMOUTH

VODKA

WHISKEY

WINE

```
M A W N J N L R J B Q Q G P
U K S H R B O T T L E E W Z
E D H P I V H B T D E X I M
F O O R P S P I R I T S S U
P V P Z E A K I Y U J C W R
H U S E A E N E F D O I Z G
H C V H T K B H Y T N B L Y
T B A T I H Y R C E J A R P
U J B N L O A H A S S R R U
O Y G I G O L N K S E L O B
M V I S T O H S O H M E U O
R L N B P E C O S L B Y Q O
E N G A P M A H C A H Q I Z
V R R O T E Q U I L A D L E
Q T R O P A O R E G A L U A
Y T Y D B D J X A M J Q D Z
```

Solution on Page 312

AIR	MAGMA
ANIMALS	MANTLE
ATMOSPHERE	MOUNTAIN
BIOLOGY	NATURE
BIOSPHERE	OCEANS
CHEMISTRY	PLANET
CHRONOLOGY	PLATES
CLIMATE	ROCKS
CORE	SOIL
CRUST	SPHERES
EARTHQUAKE	STUDY
ECOLOGY	TECTONIC
ENERGY	VOLCANOES
GEOGRAPHY	WEATHER
GEOLOGY	
GEOPHYSICS	
GEOSCIENCE	
GEOSPHERE	
GLACIOLOGY	
HYDROLOGY	
LAVA	
LIFE	

```
Y D U T S W E A T H E R O C
T H N A T U R E C O L O G Y
E N E R G Y X Y G O L O E G
T E N A L P L A T E S J F O
A G E O S P H E R E S O I L
M E S E K A U Q H T R A E O
I O C H R O N O L O G Y N I
L G I N Y E R E H P S O I B
C R S T E D H E F I L M A A
I A Y S A I R P L A V A T N
N P H U C H C O S T Q G N I
O H P R O C K S L O N M U M
T Y O C E A N S O O M A O A
C H E M I S T R Y E G T M L
E Y G O L O I C A L G Y A S
T Q B B V O L C A N O E S G
```

Solution on Page 312

ACCOUNTS

ATMS

BALANCE

BILLS

BONDS

BRANCH

BUSINESS

CAPITAL

CASH

CHANGE

CHECKING

COINS

CREDIT

CURRENCY

CUSTOMERS

DEBT

DEPOSITS

DRAFT

ECONOMY

FEES

FINANCIAL

INTEREST

INVESTMENT

LENDING

LINES

MANAGER

MONEY

MORTGAGE

NATIONAL

OVERDRAWN

PAYMENT

RATE

ROBBERY

SECURITY

TELLER

VAULT

WITHDRAWAL

```
F E E S R E L L E T H E H D
M O R T G A G E H R C Y S R
N Z G N I K C E H C N C W A
A Y T U W L A I C N A N I F
T M L O I A I N T E R E S T
I O U C L W R C L O B R E N
O N A C I A C D A S O R C E
N O V A N R U E R S Y U U M
A C S E E D S G C E H C R Y
L E N D S H T T N N V K I A
A E I E L T O O I I A O T P
T T O B L I M F K S D L Y L
I A C T I W E E U U O N A U
P R O B B E R Y N B I P E B
A A B O N D S C A T M S E L
C H A N G E R E G A N A M D
```

Solution on Page 313

ASTRONOMY

CHURCH

COMPASS

DISCOVERY

EARTH

EXPERIMENT

GALILEO

GENIUS

GEOCENTRIC

GEOMETRY

HERETIC

HISTORY

ITALIAN

JUPITER

KINEMATICS

MATH

MOON

ORBIT

PENDULUM

PHILOSOPHY

PHYSICS

PISA

PLANETS

REVOLUTION

ROMAN

SCIENTIST

SKY

STARS

SUNSPOTS

TELESCOPE

THEORIES

Galileo Galilei

```
T G E N I U S T E N A L P T
M A T H S R A T S I S K Y R
U G G E O C E N T R I C L O
L H M C X P J M W H P C Z R
U N B Y H P O S O L I H P B
D I S C O V E R Y O Z U Y I
N G E O M E T R Y Q N R M T
E K I N E M A T I C S C O E
P S S C I S Y H P M Y H N L
C E N O I T U L O V E R O E
I I E M H I S T O R Y N R S
T R A P S C I E N T I S T C
E O R A F S U N S P O T S O
R E T S N A I L A T I K A P
E H H S C O E L I L A G R E
H T B J U P I T E R O M A N
```

Solution on Page 313

ALPHABET

ANCIENT

BIBLE

CATHOLIC

CHURCH

CLASSICAL

CLERGY

CULTURE

DEAD

FORMAL

FRENCH

GRAMMAR

GREEK

HISTORICAL

INFLECTED

ITALY

LANGUAGE

LATIUM

LEGAL

LITERATURE

MASS

MEDICINE

MEDIEVAL

MUSIC

PIG

ROMANCE

ROOTS

SCHOOLS

SCIENTIFIC

SPANISH

SPOKEN

VATICAN

VOCABULARY

WRITTEN

```
F R E N C H V A T I C A N Z
S X L K Q E R U T L U C E N
C V O C A B U L A R Y H K E
B H E M I M U S I C G H O T
T I U R U F S X Y I R I P T
E E B R U I I J P N E S S I
C R B L C T T T P F L T C R
N I E A E H A A N L C O H W
A R L F H N R L E G R O L
M I A O S P I T E C I I O E
O R N M H P L C N T D C L G
R O G M M T A A I E I A S A
V O U M E A A N M D I L E L
I T A L Y C R C I R E C D D
Y S G R E E K G Y S O M N O
S M E D I E V A L E H F F A
```

Solution on Page 313

AGED

ALCOHOL

AROMA

BARREL

BODY

BOTTLE

BOUQUET

BREATHING

BURGUNDY

CABERNET

CASK

CELLAR

CHAMPAGNE

CORKSCREW

DECANTING

DRY

FINISH

FRANCE

FRENCH

FRUIT

GLASS

GRAPES

ITALY

MERLOT

NOSE

OAK

PORT

RESERVE

SANGRIA

SHERRY

SPARKLING

SWEET

TASTING

VARIETAL

VINEYARD

VINTAGE

WHITE

WINERY

YEAR

YIELD

Speaking of Wine

```
E E L T T O B X Y L A T I A
S Y D N U G R U B R G V P M
O R V A R I E T A L E I W O
N R S M B J A V S F D N H R
Y E P E A J T L R E R T I A
V H A R V K H U C E Y A T W
W S R L A I I A E O S G E H
E R K O Y T N N L B H E T C
R A L T S T G E O P A O R N
C L I G I A R U Y I J T L E
S L N N P R Q P R A A W C R
K E G M A U O G Y S R N T F
R C A B E R N E T E A D E J
O H O T T A X I G R A P E S
C D G H S I N I F W C R W V
Y I E L D G L A S S C A S K
```

Solution on Page 313

ALPACA

BUFFALO

CAMEL

CANARY

CATS

CHICKENS

COCKATIEL

DONKEYS

DOVE

DUCK

ELEPHANT

FERRET

FINCH

GEESE

GOATS

GOLDFISH

GOOSE

GUINEA PIG

HAMSTER

HONEY BEE

HORSE

LLAMA

MOUSE

PET

PIGEON

RABBIT

REINDEER

SHEEP

SWAN

TURKEY

YAK

```
W D M T L C K V Q I D F B Z
Y X C A U G O O S E C M L P
J J N H S I F D L O G T S O
I G X D T A F Q C A D B T Q
G C E E O N F K H A F U A H
U L A E D N A I A S N F C Q
I Z C B S T K H N Y X A U K
N K A Y I E S E P C M F R B
E B P E D G K S Y E H N F Y
A T L N Y C R Y L S L O E E
P L A O I R E E D N I E R K
I J S H T U A S T A O G R R
G W C O I I M B U S D I E U
I Z R R S W A N B O M P T T
G E T S T B L O V I M A T O
S H E E P E L E P E T X H N
```

Solution on Page 314

ANGER	JOY
ANXIETY	LONGING
AWE	LOVE
BORED	LUST
CONTENT	NERVOUS
DESIRE	OPTIMISM
DESPAIR	PANIC
DISGUST	PITY
ELATION	PLEASURE
EMPATHY	PRIDE
ENVY	RAGE
FEAR	RELIEF
FEELING	SADNESS
FRIGHT	SHAME
GLAD	SORROW
GLEE	SYMPATHY
GRIEF	TRUST
GUILT	ZEST
HATRED	
HOPE	
HORROR	
HURT	

```
C R G B A H A T R E D F S S
A W E L T I X Q R O T O W X
B T P L E F W I D E R O B L
H S I D I E S B Y R U R U J
G U T E A E E V O L S S O S
G L Y V D L F W J Y T U S H
F Z D P U I G Y H J W O S A
N M I A T N E T N O C V E M
O E S N V G A E X N F R N E
I T G I P P R I A P S E D G
T H U C M P F X R E G N A A
A G S E E I J N Y E G X S R
L I T K Y H T A P M Y S Y H
E R U S A E L P R I D E V F
J F E I R G V L O N G I N G
P A C Z E S T R U H O P E H
```

Solution on Page 314

ACOUSTIC

BANJO

BOWED

CELLO

CHORD

DULCIMER

ELECTRIC

FIDDLE

GUITAR

HARP

INSTRUMENT

KACAPI

KOTO

LUTES

LYRE

MANDOLIN

MUSICAL

OCTOBASS

PANDURA

PIANO

PLUCKED

REBAB

SITAR

TAMBURA

TANBUR

UKULELE

VIOLIN

ZITHER

String Instruments

```
A H K R S A R U B M A T J L
N N P E A N I L O D N A M Q
M H R E H T I Z E E R R V G
Z R C S S O I K M N U U G G
S A E I M F C U A W B D B V
Q T L M R U R T G C N N V D
A I L C I T S U O C A A N C
W S O F S C C I N B T P G N
J V E N H U L E C Q A T I J
S P I O K B D U L A P S U D
Y L R O N A I P D E L K S C
A D T A L R V E B Y U T E N
I O S J H I W A R L C F T K
V V R O R O N E E M K E U G
R E B A B J Z L R Z E B L Q
Y S N G O I E E L D D I F I
```

Solution on Page 314

ACTIVITY	MEDIA
AMUSEMENT	MONOPOLY
BOOKS	MOVIE
BOWLING	MUSICAL
CARD GAME	OPERA
CARTOONS	PEOPLE
CINEMA	PLAYS
CIRCUS	PUPPETS
CLOWNS	RADIO
COMEDY	READING
COMICS	RECREATION
CONCERT	RELAX
DANCE	SINGER
DIVERSION	SPORTS
ENJOYMENT	STORY
FILM	THEATRE
FUN	VIDEO
GAMBLING	
HOBBIES	
HUMOR	
LAUGHTER	
LEISURE	

Entertainment

```
H O B B I E S Y A L P B X Y
R E L A X M O N O P O L Y T
V A P E O P L E O W R S H R
Y I M U S I C A L O E U Y E
S D D Z P Y T I V I T C A C
C E E E B P N Q L D H R G N
I M L M O G E S H I G I A O
M S E A O R M T A V U C M C
O I I G K C E U S E A L B I
C N S D S R S A N R L O L N
S G U R T H U F D S F W I E
P E R A R O M U H I U N N M
O R E C R E A T I O N S G A
R H E N J O Y M E N T G B Q
T D A N C E I V O M L I F M
S T O R Y A R E P O I D A R
```

Solution on Page 314

PUZZLES • **89**

AUTISM	PARENTS
AUTONOMY	PHYSICAL
BABY	PLAYING
BEHAVIOR	PRESCHOOL
BIRTH	PSYCHOLOGY
BRAIN	PUBERTY
CHANGES	SKILLS
CHILDHOOD	STUDY
CHILDREN	TEACHING
COGNITIVE	TEETHING
EDUCATION	THEORIES
EMOTIONAL	TODDLER
GENETICS	
GROWTH	
INFANT	
LANGUAGE	
LEARNING	
LOVE	
MENTAL	
NEWBORN	
NURTURE	
NUTRITION	

```
G H H T R I B C H A N G E S
E L N B P R E S C H O O L T
N E R D L I H C P N I E E U
E A O L A T A T H U T V M D
T R B A Y P V N Y R I N O Y
I N W T I S I A S T R I T T
C I E N N Y O F I U T A I R
S N N E G C R N C R U R O E
P G S M J H G I A E N B N B
A N K D O O H D L I H C A U
R I I Y C L M S I T U A L P
E H L B N O I T A C U D E S
N C L A N G U A G E V O L K
T A S B C Y M O N O T U A D
S E I R O E H T O D D L E R
N T E E T H I N G R O W T H
```

Solution on Page 315

APPETIZER

ASPARAGUS

BEANS

BREADS

BROCCOLI

CABBAGE

CARROTS

CHIPS

COLESLAW

CORN

COURSE

COUSCOUS

CUISINE

DESSERT

DINNER

DRESSING

FOOD

FRIES

GREENS

LUNCH

MEAL

MUSHROOMS

PASTAS

PEAS

PLATE

PORTION

POTATOES

RESTAURANT

RICE

ROLLS

SALADS

SAUCE

SERVING

SMALL BOWL

SOUPS

SQUASH

STARCH

STUFFING

VEGETABLES

```
E H C N U L N O I T R O P X
T C U A S T A R C H C D V H
B S I K P C L C A R R O T S
R N S R O P O T A T O E S E
E E I R R L E B D I N N E R
A E N V E G E T A B L E S V
D R E S S I N G I W Y E M I
S G L T T S C D O Z G E O N
L A E M A O C B O A E B O G
W S U E U L L O B O S R R N
S N P R R L P B U A F O H I
O A S P A R A G U S L C S F
U E T M N C S C N L C C U F
P B S S T R E S S E D O M U
S D A L A S Q U A S H L U T
O O S I S P I H C F R I E S
```

Solution on Page 315

ADDRESS	POST CARDS
ADHESIVE	POSTMARK
AIRMAIL	PRICE
BOOKLET	ROLL
COLLECTOR	SEND
COST	SHEETS
COUNTRY	SMALL
DELIVERY	STICK
DESIGNS	USPS
ENVELOPE	
FOREVER	
GOVERNMENT	
HOBBY	
LETTERS	
LICK	
MAILING	
METER	
PACKAGE	
PAPER	
PERFORATED	
PHILATELY	
PICTURE	

```
A R S K E C I R P M U X F R
P I C T U R E A S E P I I C
O D R O L L C P S T E E H S
S T E M Y K E O N E R B X T
T E A L A L P S G R F G U I
M L S G I I O T I J O N S C
A K E C I V L C S V R I P K
R O K X C Q E A E G A L S C
K O E Y C A V R D U T I M C
O B T V S E N D Y F E A A Q
T S O C I M E S O Z D M L J
A D D R E S S R E T T E L P
H D K N Y L E T A L I H P I
R T T B G V L H O B B Y F Q
M P A P E R D O D X N L V C
U T Y R T N U O C A I V Y A
```

Solution on Page 315

APPS	MOVIES
AUDIO	MULTITOUCH
BATTERY	MUSIC
BUSINESS	PHOTOS
COMPUTER	POPULAR
DESIGN	PORTABLE
DEVICE	SAFARI
DISPLAY	SCREEN
EBOOKS	SOFTWARE
ELECTRONIC	STEVE JOBS
GADGET	TABLET
GAMES	TECHNOLOGY
INNOVATION	VIDEO
INTERNET	WEB
IPHONE	WIFI
IPOD	WIRELESS
ITUNES	
JAILBREAK	
LAPTOP	
MAC	
MEDIA	
MOBILE	

```
S M H M J W I R E L E S S Z
C P O C K A E R B L I A J T
R R P B U I N T E R N E T E
E E Y A I O S C P O T P A L
E T A S Y L T Y R E T T A B
N U L I G R E I E O I D U A
O P P N O A V P T C M S P T
E M S N L L E O M L I V A R
D O I O O U J D W N U V T O
I C D V N P O B E I S M E P
V I M A H O B S B R K D G D
I S O T C P S C Z A O E D G
F U V I E R A W T F O S A A
I M I O T M E D I A B I G M
W A E N O H P I C S E G O E
B M S O T O H P I T U N E S
```

Solution on Page 315

ANIMAL

AQUARIUMS

AURELIA

BEACH

BLOOMS

CLEAR

COLORFUL

CUBOZOA

CURRENTS

DEADLY

DEEP SEA

FIRST AID

FISH

FLOATING

FOOD

FRESHWATER

GELATINOUS

JELLIES

MEDUSOZOA

NATURE

OCEAN

ORGANISM

PAINFUL

POISON

RED

SCYPHOZOA

SMALL

SOFT

STAUROZOA

STINGING

SWARMS

SWIMMING

TENTACLES

TOXIC

UMBRELLA

VINEGAR

```
T O X I C F L O A T I N G T
G A D U M B R E L L A M S F
O B L O O M S I N A G R O O
D E R F O P G N I M M I W S
S A I R E F S F N A T U R E
W C G E L A T I N O U S C I
A H D S M U I R A U Q A U L
R P E H C R N S O R A O B L
M A A W L E G T Z A N Z O E
S I D A E L I A O G I O Z J
G N L T A I N I H E M S O N
O F Y E R A G D P N A U A O
C U R R E N T S Y I L D H S
E L U F R O L O C V A E S I
A O Z O R U A T S A F M I O
N X S E L C A T N E T S F P
```

Solution on Page 316

ADOBE

ALGORITHMS

APPLE

BUSINESS

CODE

COMPUTER

DATA

DISK

DOWNLOAD

DRIVERS

FIRMWARE

FREEWARE

FUNCTION

GAMES

HARDWARE

INSTALL

INTERFACE

JAVA

LANGUAGE

LINUX

MAC

MEMORY

MICROSOFT

MIDDLEWARE

OFFICE

PHOTOSHOP

PROCEDURES

PROGRAMS

SHAREWARE

SYNTAX

SYSTEM

TOOLS

USER

WINDOWS

WORD

100

Computer Software

```
I P U T O O L S Y S T E M E
N F R E E W A R E M L I S C
S S C O M P U T E R D E W I
T J E C C W P M A D M I T F
A F B C O E O V L A N U U F
L I O R A R D E G D S N E O
L R D S Y F W U O E C D R T
W M A S O A R W R T D A A J
V W P S R R S E I E I O W A
D A R E D O C O T N S L E V
R R O N G A N I H N K N R A
I E G I P P C A M G I W A P
V J R S M P O H S O T O H P
E G A U G N A L A T A D S L
R D M B H A R D W A R E M E
S U S Y N T A X U N I L Q L
```

Solution on Page 316

BRAN

CHEERIOS

CLUSTERS

CORN POPS

CORNFLAKES

CRISPIX

CRUNCHY

FIBER ONE

FRUITY

GRANOLA

HONEY NUT

HONEYCOMB

KASHI

KELLOGG'S

KIX

LIFE

MUESLI

OATMEAL

PEBBLES

POST

RICE CHEX

SPECIAL K

SUGAR POPS

TOTAL

TRIX

WHEAT CHEX

WHEATIES

Breakfast Cereals

```
Y T G E H W J S B X P Z M G
T U N I O A T M E A L F D I
I X A K G S O I R E E H C E
U C R U N C H Y K I X E F M
R W B L Y P C N X E C I G C
F I B E R O N E H X L R R S
V D N S Q X H C I T U I E L
N O I U M C E R U S S I S A
H K L G T C N E P T P P T
I A S A I S Y L I A E U O O
E S E R O E B X E C R M P T
O H U P N B K H I V S K N I
W I M O E J W A L O N A R G
Q M H P K E L L O G G S O P
Z E X S E K A L F N R O C X
P N B C G U K W R Q U P S I
```

Solution on Page 316

APPLIANCES

ASSOCIATES

BLUE

BUSINESS

CAMERAS

CELL PHONE

COMPUTERS

CONSUMER

CUSTOMERS

DRYERS

DVD PLAYER

ELECTRONIC

EXPENSIVE

GADGETS

GAMES

GEEK SQUAD

MEDIA

MOVIE

MUSIC

ONLINE

PHONES

RETAILER

SALES

SERVICE

SHOPPING

SOFTWARE

STEREO

STORE

TECHNOLOGY

TELEVISION

TVS

WARRANTY

YELLOW TAG

Best Buy

```
C S R Y T N A R R A W S B E
S E E N I L N O P S A T L V
O N M T S Q R P R L O E U I
F O U A A E L E E H C C E S
T H S B O I M S T T D H C N
W P N P A O C A R A Z N C E
A L O N T Z A O G J I O A P
R L C S S E N I S U B L M X
E E U E C I V R E S S O E E
S C Y E C S T E G D A G R R
F X D A U Q S K E E G Y A O
Y Y E L L O W T A G T V S E
S R E T U P M O C I S U M R
E I V O M E D I A S T O R E
F I N O I S I V E L E T S T
S H O P P I N G D R Y E R S
```

Solution on Page 316

AESTHETIC

BASEBALL

BERMUDA

CARE

CUT

DIRT

EDGE

FERTILIZER

FLOWERS

FOOTBALL

GARDENS

GOLF

GRASSES

GREEN

GROW

HOME

HOUSE

INSECTS

IRRIGATE

LANDSCAPE

LAWN MOWER

MOWING

PARKS

PESTICIDE

PLANTING

SEEDS

SERVICE

SHRUBS

SOIL

SPRINKLER

SUMMER

TENNIS

TREES

TRIM

TURF

WATERING

WEED

YARD

```
Y H L Y S G Z B T H B F K Y
U G O L V R A G R O W L E O
P W R M A S E R I U Y O B N
H E I A E B S W D S S W E T
H D S B S T T E O E F E R F
K P A T C S H O E M N R M E
Y L Q E I V E R O D N S U R
L A S Q N C T S D F S W D T
I N R S P R I N K L E R A I
I T S D O L C D W O R S C L
G I R R I G A T E G V K U I
G N I R E T A W I M I R T Z
R G I R H L A N D S C A P E
E G A W S H R U B S E P D R
E C L I O S I N N E T G Q L
N C S U M M E R W E E D K A
```

Solution on Page 317

APPETIZER

BACON BITS

BOWL

CAESAR

CARROTS

CHEESE

CHICKEN

COBB

CROUTONS

CUCUMBERS

DRESSING

EGGS

FRESH

FRUIT

GREENS

HAM

HEALTHY

ITALIAN

LETTUCE

MEAT

NUTS

OLIVES

ONIONS

PASTA

PEPPERS

PLATE

POTATO

RADISH

RANCH

ROMAINE

SAUCE

SEAFOOD

SIDE DISH

SPINACH

TOMATOES

TOSSED

TUNA

VEGETABLES

VINEGAR

Toss a Salad

```
E C U A S W D H J P S Y A S
R I H O N I O N S O H T S P
G R E E N S O N U T S N G E
V A T G E K F B L A O P C P
I D A G H S A A P T T U A P
N I L S S G E C U O C P S E
E S P R I H S O J U P E E R
G H T A D Z R N M E L D O S
A E I S E C C B T B R L T N
R C U E D H E I A E I O A C
O U R A I R Z T S V R I M O
M T F C S E E S E R L W O B
A T K R R G I S A A N U T B
I E Y M E N K C T O S S E D
N L K V G S P I N A C H A M
E U R A N C H M E A T U N C
```

Solution on Page 317

AGATE

AGGIE

ALLEY

BALL

CAT'S EYE

CHILDREN

CIRCLE

CLAY

COLLECTING

COLORS

DESIGN

DIRT

FLICK

FOR KEEPS

GAMES

GLASS

HIT

KEEPSIES

LOSE

NOSTALGIA

PLAY

POCKET

QUITSIES

RINGER

ROLLING

ROUND

SHOOTER

SIZE

SMALL

SPHERICAL

STEEL

STONE

SWIRL

TAKE

TARGET

THUMB

TOYS

TRADE

WIN

Marbles

```
N G I S E D N U O R T U U Y
T P T E K C O P E I G G A P
O N R I S I R S H N G G L Z
Y H I S L M E T A G A A L X
S A D P P R A L L E Y E E X
E Q S E C H I L D R E N X E
M P E E N L E W L T G S H W
A I I K Y O A R S N Q T E I
G Q S I Z E S Y I R O O K C
L N T P T J S T E C T N A S
A I I H E R C T A R A E T G
S W U L O E O F A L L L E H
S M Q L L O K D R C G S G S
B A O L H O E R R E O I R F
M C O S V K R I O L L L A B
Q C R F L I C K J F O X T U
```

Solution on Page 317

PUZZLES • 111

ACTIVITIES	PARENT
ADDITION	PLAY
ART	PRESCHOOL
BLOCKS	PRINCIPAL
BOOKS	READING
BUS	SINGING
CENTERS	SKILLS
CHILDHOOD	SOCIAL
CHILDREN	SONGS
CLASSROOM	STORY
DRAWING	STUDENTS
EDUCATION	TEACHERS
ELEMENTARY	VOCABULARY
FUN	WRITING
INTERACT	YOUNG
KIDS	
LANGUAGE	
LEARNING	
LINE	
MATH	
MUSIC	
NUMBERS	

Kindergarten

```
I N T E R A C T M S O N G S
G C H I L D H O O D F T G Y
N H N O M E O G N I T I R W
I S O A U R M S L L I K S A
G K I W S T N E D U T S J C
N C T S I U L A N G U A G E
I O A A C T I V I T I E S N
S L C V O C A B U L A R Y T
C B U Y O U N G O G M R K E
H A D D I T I O N P J A Y R
I Q E N I L H I K I D S T S
L L A P I C N I R P W A N H
D Y A Z S R E B M U N A E P
R A T E A C H E R S T O R Y
E L R E A D I N G F U N A D
N P L A I C O S K O O B P F
```

Solution on Page 317

AGE
ART FORM
ARTISTIC
BARK
CARE
CHINESE
DWARFING
FORMS
GARDEN
GRAFTING
GREEN
GROWTH
HISTORY
HOBBY
INDOOR
JAPANESE
JUNIPER
LEAVES
MINIATURE
NATURE
NURSERY
OLD

OUTDOOR
PENJING
PERENNIAL
PINE
PLANTING
POTTED
PRUNING
SAMURAI
SHAPING
SHRUB
SOIL
STYLES
TOOLS
TREES
TRIMMING
WATER
WIRING
ZEN

Bonsai

```
S  M  C  H  I  N  E  S  E  N  A  P  A  J
E  Y  G  M  T  R  E  E  S  U  E  O  H  M
L  R  G  N  I  N  U  R  P  R  B  Z  J  K
Y  O  U  A  I  D  L  O  E  S  G  J  U  G
T  T  B  T  B  J  W  N  E  E  R  G  N  N
S  S  A  U  A  O  N  A  E  R  A  C  I  I
C  I  R  R  P  I  N  E  R  Y  F  C  P  T
I  H  K  E  A  C  N  D  P  F  T  M  E  N
S  T  S  L  S  R  C  I  T  S  I  T  R  A
L  W  L  N  A  Z  T  G  M  R  N  N  A  L
E  O  O  S  M  R  O  F  O  K  G  T  G  P
A  R  O  O  U  T  D  O  O  R  Z  E  E  O
V  G  T  I  R  Y  D  G  A  R  D  E  N  T
E  S  N  L  A  N  G  N  I  M  M  I  R  T
S  H  A  P  I  N  G  N  I  R  I  W  M  E
W  A  T  E  R  H  O  B  B  Y  J  Z  M  D
```

Solution on Page 318

APPLIANCES

AUTOMOTIVE

BEDDING

BUSINESS

CATALOG

CHAIN

CHICAGO

CLOTHING

CRAFTSMAN

CREDIT

DEPARTMENT

FURNITURE

HARDWARE

HOUSEWARES

JEWELRY

KENMORE

KMART

LAWN MOWER

MAIL ORDER

MALLS

MOWERS

OLD

PAINT

REPAIR

RETAILER

ROEBUCK

SALES

SERVICE

SHOPPING

STORES

SUPPLIES

TOOLS

TOWER

TOYS

WISHBOOK

Solution on Pag

```
T R A M K E R U T I N R U F
N T J C O R E L I A T E R R
B O S H O P P I N G S D R O
G Y S I B S G T I D E R C E
O S E C H R N S F P H O T B
L E N A S E I E A E O L O U
A C I G I W H R P C U I W C
T N S O W O T O A I S A E K
A A U T O M O T I V E M R B
C I B L E N L S N R W A A E
H L D N F W C U T E A L W D
A P T R I A P E R S R L D D
I P S E I L P P U S E S R I
N A S O H C R A F T S M A N
J E W E L R Y S A L E S H G
S L O O T E R O M N E K D N
```

Solution on Page 318

AEROSPACE	SAFETY
ANALYSIS	SOFTWARE
BRIDGES	STRUCTURES
BUILDING	SYSTEMS
CHEMICAL	TECHNICAL
COLLEGE	TECHNOLOGY
COMPUTERS	TRAIN
CONSTRUCT	UNIVERSITY
EDUCATION	WORK
INDUSTRIAL	
INGENUITY	
JOB	
KNOWLEDGE	
MATERIALS	
MECHANICS	
PHYSICS	
PLAN	
PROBLEMS	
PRODUCTION	
PROFESSION	
REGULATION	
RESEARCH	

```
S B S L Y G O L O N H C E T
A U E A U M P R O B L E M S F
F I G I S L A I R E T A M W
E L D R N S T B O J N Q A O
T D I T A A H C R A E S E R
Y I R S L C O L L E G E R K
T N B U P P H Y S I C S O T
I G G D S Y S T E M S T S K
S E S N O I T C U D O R P N
R N O I S S E F O R P U A O
E U F O L A C I M E H C C W
V I T C O N S T R U C T E L
I T W C I N O I T A C U D E
N Y A A C O M P U T E R S D
U T R C L A C I N H C E T G
I T E M E C H A N I C S O E
```

Solution on Page 318

AGE

ANIMAL

AQUATIC

BEACH

BOX TURTLE

CARAPACE

CLAWS

CRAWL

EGGS

ENDANGERED

FLIPPERS

GREEN

HARE

HIDE

LAND

MARINE

NATURE

NECK

OCEAN

OLD

PETS

REPTILES

SEA TURTLE

SHELLS

SHIELD

SLOW

SNAPPING

SOUP

SPECIES

SWIMMING

TAIL

TERRAPIN

TORTOISE

WATER

ZOO

120

Turtle Life

```
C P C D F S E I C E P S Y N
O J Y E N M G C I T A U Q A
R B D E R E G N A D N E C T
L I L L E L E E I P N O M U
H O O T S T I R C M A A T R
N H O R I R T A G P M R L E
P A Z U O U E H T T M I A X
P F V T T T E P U R G D W C
Q E M A R X R E P T I L E S
J W T E O O D L E I H S L N
L S A S T B A H E N L L T A
R O C T H G F N C G E F R P
G U C R E C I L I H G C W P
W P H E A R A B S M W S K I
F U K E A W T E R R A P I N
E T P M S N L C B W O L S G
```

Solution on Page 318

Puzzles • **121**

ASPHALT

BUILDING

CHIMNEY

COLLAPSE

COVERING

DRAINAGE

DURABILITY

DWELLING

EAVES

FELT

FLAT

GABLE

GUTTERS

HOUSE

INSULATION

MATERIAL

METAL

NAILS

PEAKED

PITCH

PROTECTS

REPAIR

REPLACE

ROOFER

SHINGLES

SLATE

SLOPE

SNOW

SOLAR

STRAW

TAR

THATCHING

TILES

TOP

WEATHER

WOOD

122

Roofs

```
T A L F G D T B A L W O O D
I T F O Y E N M I H C G B E
L L A I R E T A M O N W U K
E A V E S G R O V I O M I A
S H V Y N A S E H G A B L E
W P S C T N R C W J J E D P
A S H N O I T A L U S N I I
R A I W N A L N L P Q L N T
T O N G H R J I A O J L G C
S C G T L D W L B I S N C H
L R L P T E L E C A L P E R
A L E O A O P R Z L R S E E
T A S T C E T O R P T U P P
E T H R T G N I L L E W D A
U E A H O U S E E S S H S I
R M Q S V C G F R O O F E R
```

Solution on Page 319

ATTACK	QUEEN
BISHOPS	ROOKS
BLACK	RULES
BOARD GAME	SKILL
CAPTURE	SQUARES
CASTLING	STALEMATE
CHAMPION	STRATEGY
CHECKERED	TACTICS
CHECKMATE	THINKING
CHESSBOARD	TURN
CLUB	WHITE
COMPUTER	WIN
FORK	
FUN	
GAMBIT	
KINGS	
KNIGHTS	
MASTERS	
MOVES	
OPPONENT	
PAWNS	
PIECES	

The Game of Kings

```
B O A R D G A M E R P N T O
C A P T U R E E I W I N A O
F B L N E T A M K C E H C A
P A W N S E V O M C C E T J
X S S P O H S I B A E T I D
A C M A S T E R S S S A C E
T E T I H W C K S T S M S R
T K V G K R O F K L E E H E
A I I V U O M R O I R L H K
C N C H A M P I O N A A K C
K G B H N J U P R G U T G E
Z S S L Q E T E O J Q S A H
N S T R A T E G Y N S R M C
R U L E S C R U H N E E B L
U R Z L L I K S Q F U N I U
T U S C U G N I K N I H T B
```

Solution on Page 319

ACCENT

ARTIFICIAL

BRIGHT

BULBS

CANDLES

CEILING

DARK

DAYLIGHT

DIM

ELECTRICAL

FILAMENT

FIXTURE

FLOODLIGHT

FLOOR LAMP

GLOW

HALOGEN

ILLUMINATE

INDOOR

LAMPS

LANTERN

LED

LIGHT BULB

NATURAL

NEON

NIGHT

OUTDOOR

RECESSED

SCONCE

SEE

SHADOW

SHOW

SOLAR

SPOTLIGHT

STAGE

SUN

SWITCH

TRACK

VIEW

WATT

WIRING

```
E C N O C S H A D O W L L S
W R S F C A N D L E S Z A B
O E U P L V I E W P L G R L
L T H T M O R O O D N I U U
G A Z C X A O T D I M N T B
L N T L T I L D R E B O A J
P I E H A I F I L A M E N T
O M G G G I W E E I D N N H
K U A H A I C S G T G T R A
C L T L T T R I Y H D H E L
A L N D R B S B F G Y G T O
R I E I O O U C E I L I N G
T C C N K O O L C L T N A E
K A C R U D R L B Y U R L N
L R A L O S E E F A T T A W
U D R E C E S S E D W O H S
```

Solution on Page 319

BALD

BARBER

BLACK

BLOND

BODY

BROWN

BUN

CLIP

COMB

CONDITION

CURLY

CUTTING

DERMIS

DYE

EYELASHES

FINE

FOLLICLES

GEL

GRAY

GROWTH

HAIRCUT

HEAD

KERATIN

LENGTH

LONG

PERMANENT

RED

ROOT

SCALP

SCISSORS

SET

SHAVING

SHORT

SOFT

STRAIGHT

STYLE

TEXTURE

WASH

WAVY

WIGS

Hair

```
B H I H L H C G X M S L Y G
W A V Y S U U N L Z O E C R
I P L A C S H A V I N G T O
G G W D K E R A T I N F H W
S V K Z X D E O C N O T G T
G S Z C A N B U S S W N I H
N H J E A O R G N S I O A V
O O H L D L A U E T I I R P
L R I Y Y B B H T L R C T B
C T E T A N S U T C O O S D
F H S S I A C E U G A M T D
Q T L I L D X T Q R A B E B
E G O E M T N E N A M R E P
X N Y O U R Y O D Y E K I Y
P E I R R S E L C I L L O F
D L E F L B U D M A C T Q U
```

Solution on Page 319

ALIENS

AMBUSH

ARCADE

ASTEROIDS

ATARI

BATMAN

BATTLEZONE

CENTIPEDE

COMMANDO

CONTRA

CRAZY TAXI

DEFENDER

DIG DUG

DUCK HUNT

FROGGER

GALAXIAN

GAUNTLET

JOUST

MAPPY

MARIO BROS.

METAL SLUG

PACMAN

PINBALL

PLAY

PONG

QIX

SIMPSONS

STAR WARS

TEKKEN

TETRIS

TRON

130

Classic Arcade Games

```
N E L S O R B O I R A M J A
W T E K K E N G X I Q G P Z
H N A M C A P U A M B U S H
L U E N O Z E L T T A B S D
R H T E T R I S Y C F D R I
E K A S O I J L Z Y I I A X
D C L I I R X A A O P P W L
N U I M I A R T R D I P R I
E D E P I T N E C N G W A D
F J N S N A T M B A A R T M
E P S O M S P A L M U E S E
D O C N A P L A Y M N D U V
Q N N S Y L X W M O T A O D
R G U D G I D B Y C L C J K
A C S G A F R O G G E R I Q
T R O N A M T A B C T A M G
```

Solution on Page 320

HICCUPS

HICKEYS

HICKORY

HIDINGS

HIGH ROAD

HIGHEST

HIGHLIFE

HIGHNESS

HIGHTAIL

HIGHWAYS

HIKING

HILARITY

HILLERS

HILLIEST

HILLSIDE

HILLTOPS

HILTING

HIMSELF

HINDMOST

HINTING

HIPBONES

HIPLINES

HIPSHOT

HIPSTERS

HIRABLE

HIRELING

HIRING

HISSINGS

HITCHING

HITHERTO

HIVELESS

```
S  R  E  L  L  I  H  I  M  S  E  L  F  C
T  S  E  I  L  L  I  H  I  C  K  O  R  Y
S  H  L  Y  T  I  R  A  L  I  H  J  D  P
S  I  B  S  U  A  T  S  E  H  G  I  H  S
E  P  A  Y  T  T  S  O  M  D  N  I  H  T
L  S  R  A  G  H  I  L  L  T  O  P  S  X
E  T  I  W  S  G  N  I  S  S  I  H  E  H
V  E  H  H  H  I  P  B  O  N  E  S  N  I
I  R  F  G  Q  H  I  C  C  U  P  S  I  T
H  S  T  I  H  I  T  H  E  R  T  O  L  C
I  Y  O  H  L  G  N  I  T  L  I  H  P  H
D  E  H  I  G  H  N  E  S  S  O  F  I  I
I  K  S  K  K  R  G  N  I  T  N  I  H  N
N  C  P  I  E  O  H  I  R  E  L  I  N  G
G  I  I  N  F  A  S  C  H  I  R  I  N  G
S  H  H  G  E  D  I  S  L  L  I  H  N  V
```

Solution on Page 320

ACROBATICS

APPLES

AUDIENCE

BALLS

BEANBAGS

CATCHING

CHAINSAWS

CIRCUS

CLOWN

CLUBS

FESTIVAL

FIRE

HANDS

HOBBY

JESTER

JUGGLERS

KNIVES

MOTION

OBJECTS

PERFORMER

PROP

RHYTHM

RINGS

SHOW

SKILL

SPORTS

THROWING

TORCHES

TOSS

TRICKS

```
Y N R S C I T A B O R C A G
P N X S G H R A S E V I N K
R P C E H U A B W S K I L L
L E F H O O C I Q X W M L M
P I M C P G W I N O N P A Z
H Y O R C M N X R S I X V D
V A O O O A J H I C A G I S
B P P T A F T F V Z U W T T
R U I P J C R C I I D S S C
I O O Q L U R E H R I A E E
N G K O S E G D P I E F F J
G X W L T M S G A B N A E B
S N L S R S B U L C C G U O
X A E H O B B Y X E E R P Q
B J I T P M H T Y H R R T D
H A N D S V T R I C K S A T
```

Solution on Page 320

ASSONANCE	POETS
BALLAD	PROSE
BEAUTIFUL	READING
BOOKS	RHYMING
CLASSIC	RHYTHM
COLLECTION	ROMANCE
COUPLET	SIMILE
DRAMA	SONNET
EPIC	STANZAS
FEELINGS	STORY
FREE VERSE	TEXT
HAIKU	THOUGHTS
IAMBIC	TONE
LANGUAGE	VERSES
LIMERICK	WHITMAN
LINES	WORDS
LITERATURE	WRITING
LOVE	
LYRICS	
MEANING	
METER	
ODES	

```
H R E E S O R P O E T S N E
S E N I L I M E R I C K U P
P T O S E C N A M O R W W I
W E T C O B A L L A D R R C
F M E I F D E L I M I S I S
S E S R E V E E R F S B T T
P A E Y U C E S S T M E I O
R S S L T T G T H A C A N R
W S K I I E A G I S L U G Y
R O O M K N U R O F A T N L
H N O T Z O G N E E S I I D
Y A B A H U N S V T S F M R
T N S T K E A O V J I U Y A
H C X I T E L P U O C L H M
M E A N I N G N I D A E R A
T H S D R O W H I T M A N E
```

Solution on Page 320

BAGELS	NEW YORK
BOLOGNA	NUMBER
BREAD	OLIVES
CAVIAR	ORDER
CHEESES	PASTRAMI
CHICKEN	PICKLE
COFFEE	SALAMI
COLD CUTS	SANDWICHES
COOKIES	SAUSAGE
COUNTER	SHOP
DELICIOUS	STORE
DIPS	TEA
DRINKS	TUNA
FINE FOODS	TURKEY
GERMAN	WINE
GROCERY	
HAM	
JEWISH	
KOSHER	
LUNCH	
MEATS	
MILK	

Delicatessen

```
S Y T G L I M A R T S A P O
K O S H E R K S N U M B E R
C O O K I E S P O G C K N D
Q U F R N B Y I S D O W I E
F P T O D I C D A H F L W R
T I U Y K I R E N A F S O J
D C N W L E R D D M E N E B
H K A E T B N S W V E W R P
G L D N F C T Z I K I A V O
R E U X A O K L C S E E T H
O O N V R L O I H T G S N S
C U I E I D H D E A L A N H
E A Z M D C S E S E E H C C
R Y E K R U T U G E R M A N
Y B B U G T A A W F U K E U
I M A L A S B K C B E H M L
```

Solution on Page 321

APERTURE

ASPECT

CAMERA

CANON

CAPTURE

CARD

COMPUTERS

CROPPING

DELETE

DOWNLOAD

EASY

EDITING

EXPOSURE

FILTER

FLASH

FOCUS

IMAGING

INTERNET

KODAK

LANDSCAPE

LENS

LIGHT

MEGAPIXEL

MEMORY

OLYMPUS

PICTURES

PIXELS

PRINTING

RAW

SCANNING

SENSOR

SHARE

SIZING

SLR

SOFTWARE

SONY

STORAGE

UPLOAD

VIEW

ZOOM

Digital Photography

```
Y N O S F T E N R E T N I R
Q S F I L T E R X L E N S O
W S A M A R D P A F O C U S
C C W E S M O O Z W E I V N
R A W M H S W C A P T U R E
W N J O U I N G C C T F P S
P N H R C K L R S C A N O N
G I E Y O B O O L Y M P U S
W N C D M P A P E R T U R E
I G A T P P D E X G E S G E
T K A I U P P R I N T I N G
H C N R T R W A P I E Z I A
G G E D E U E H A T L I G R
I W R P R M H S G I E N A O
L A N D S C A P E D D G M T
C U P L O A D C M E I Y I S
```

Solution on Page 321

ACTION

AUDIO

BACKUP

BLANK

BLU-RAY

BURN

CASE

COMPACT

COMPUTER

DATA

DIGITAL

DISK

DRIVE

DVD PLAYER

FILM

FORMAT

HOME

LASER

MEDIUM

MOVIES

MUSIC

NETFLIX

OPTICAL

PAUSE

PHILIPS

PLASTIC

RECORDABLE

RENTAL

ROUND

SCRATCH

SHOW

SONY

SPEED

STORAGE

TECHNOLOGY

TELEVISION

TOSHIBA

VHS

VIDEO

WATCH

```
X T O S H I B A K S I D J M
C Z E G A R O T S E E Q H L
O X H C T A R C S E S M C I
M I G P H I L I P S R U T F
P L H S O N Y S R U Z S A V
A F T A M R O F E C K I W P
C T P R E S A L C C I C C S
T E L E V I S I O N S R A D
K N A L B S L M R G E C S B
M U A C N D P Y D Y Y I E M
E V E C R U L L A C I T P O
D I G I T A L L B R A S N V
I D V E T I P W L O U A R I
U E R N O D O Y E U D L U E
M O E Z V H S N F N I P B S
S R N D S P A T A D O Z O D
```

Solution on Page 321

AZTECS	MEXICO
BIOFUEL	MILL
CEREAL	OIL
COOK	PLANT
CORNMEAL	POPCORN
CROP	SEASON
CULTIVATE	SEEDS
EARS	STAPLE
ETHANOL	STARCH
FARMING	SWEET CORN
FIELDS	TASSEL
FOOD	TORTILLA
GENETICS	TRADE
GRAIN	VARIETIES
GRITS	VEGETABLE
GROUND	YELLOW
HARVEST	
HOMINY	
HUSK	
INDIAN	
KERNELS	
MAYANS	

```
T N A I D N I H U S K N C T
R T S L H C R A T S T I R G
A L A E M N R O C X A D O Z
D I V S E S N U C L F K P E
E O E S K D L A L P E F M V
B N G A S T S I Z R O L A Y
I R E T I C T E N T F P Y E
O O T V A R I E T I E S A L
F C A P O R L T E H A C N L
U T B T C S F L E G A R S O
E E L S I C D Y L N Z N G W
L E E E X S N D T I E A O J
P W R A E I U S N M M G C L
A S T S M A O H A R V E S T
T A K O O C R L L A E R E C
S F H N V R G S P F O O D N
```

Solution on Page 321

ACTIVITIES	NETWORKING
ADVERTISE	ONLINE
BEBO	PEOPLE
BLOG	PICTURES
CHAT	PLATFORM
CLASSMATES	PRIVACY
COMMENTS	SHARING
COMMUNITY	TECHNOLOGY
COMPUTER	TWITTER
CONNECTION	WALL
CONTACT	WEBSITE
DATING	
E-MAIL	
EVENTS	
FACEBOOK	
FRIENDSTER	
INTERACT	
INTERESTS	
INTERNET	
LIKE	
LINKEDIN	
MYSPACE	

```
L G B C O N T A C T E K I L
L C L Y K S T S E R E T N I
A H O A D V E R T I S E I N
W A G M R E T U P M O C E K
R T D P M J G N I R A H S E
M E Y I W E B S I T E N O D
Y R T C O N N E C T I O N I
S E I T I V I T C A N L E N
P T N U I H I A S D T O T P
A S U R E W N M T A E G W R
C D M E N O T S N T R Y O I
E N M S I B E S E I A L R V
P E O P L E R A V N C I K A
Q I C K N B N L E G T A I C
C R K O O B E C A F D M N Y
Y F M R O F T A L P J E G K
```

Solution on Page 322

BRIDGES	MEDICINE
BRUSHING	MOLAR
CAVITIES	ORAL
CHAIR	PAIN
CLEANING	PATIENT
CROWNS	PLAQUE
DECAY	PREVENTION
DENTIST	ROOT CANAL
DENTURES	SEDATION
DIAGNOSIS	SPIT
DISEASES	SURGERY
DOCTOR	TOOTHACHE
DRILLS	TREATMENT
EXTRACTION	
FEAR	
FILLINGS	
FLOSSING	
FLUORIDE	
GINGIVITIS	
GUM	
HEALTH	
HYGIENISTS	

```
T H T L A E H R M Y A C E D
S U R G E R Y O U T L Y D I
I S L S O M G O G R P A I N
T N S T N O I T N E V E R P
N W C P D P E C I A S H O O
E O A L I A N A S T E C U O
D R V A S T I N S M R A L I
C C I Q E I S A O E U H F W
N H T U A E T L L N T T D C
O A I E S N S I F T N O R L
I I E Z E T Z J V J E O I E
T R S I S O N G A I D T L A
A R A E F I L L I N G S L N
D F E X T R A C T I O N S I
E N I C I D E M O L A R I N
S E G D I R B R U S H I N G
```

Solution on Page 322

BAR

BICYCLE

CLOSED

CYLINDER

DEADBOLT

DEVICE

DOOR LOCKS

ELECTRONIC

ENTRY

FASTENING

GUARD

KEYCARD

KEYCODE

LOCKSMITH

LUGGAGE

MAGNETIC

MASTER

MECHANICAL

METAL

OPEN

PADLOCK

PASSWORD

PICKING

PIN LOCK

PREVENT

PRIVACY

PROTECT

RFID

SAFETY

SECRET

SECURITY

STEEL

THIEF

TUMBLER

TURN

VAULT

YALE

```
L E E T S Y V E M A S T E R
Q N C C P A D L O C K C I F
D T M A G N E T I C E E R I
O R R E D N I L Y C Y T E D
O Y C L H T I M S K C O L K
R C G K C O L N I P A R B E
L A C I N A H C E M R P M Y
O V G U D Y N R U T D D U C
C I N O R T C E L E S R T O
K R I T O I T L O B D A E D
S P K E W R N C U P E U F E
A V C R S U E Y X G E G K S
F A I C S C V C B R G N Y O
E U P E A E E I M E T A L L
T L M S P S R B A R L U G C
Y T H I E F P E D E V I C E
```

Solution on Page 322

AGES

AMERICAN

ANCIENT

ART

BOOKS

CIVIL WAR

CLASS

COUNTRIES

CULTURE

ERA

EVENTS

GOVERNMENT

HISTORIANS

KINGS

KNOWLEDGE

LEARNING

LESSONS

MILITARY

MODERN

MUSEUM

NARRATIVE

NATIONAL

OLD

PAST

PEOPLE

PERIODS

POLITICS

PREHISTORY

RECORD

RELIGION

REVOLUTION

SCHOOL

STORIES

STUDY

TIME

WARS

WESTERN

WORLD

```
P E O P L E L A N O I T A N
B R S T G O L D R O C E R A
O U N C N O I T U L O V E R
O T O T I E V E N T S J L R
K L S N N T M U E S U M I A
S U S E R A I N Y P O H G T
G C E I A W G L R D Q I I I
N I L C E D M E O E U S O V
I V N N L P H Y S P V T N E
K I N A C I R E M A P O S W
C L A S S A S M Y S E R G E
I W R T T C O U N T R I E S
N A O I H D T I M E I A R T
W R L O E G D E L W O N K E
Y I O R J G W O R L D S R R
M L N X S T O R I E S A G N
```

Solution on Page 322

ADDICTION	HYPER
ALERTNESS	JITTERS
ALKALOID	JOLT
AWAKE	KOLA NUT
BEANS	LATTE
BITTER	LEAVES
BUZZ	MOLECULE
CAPPUCCINO	PILLS
CHEMICAL	PLANT
CHOCOLATE	POP
COCA COLA	RED BULL
COFFEE	SLEEP
CUP	SODA
DECAF	SOFT DRINK
DIURETIC	STIMULANT
DRINKS	TEA
DRUG	WITHDRAWAL
ENERGY	
ESPRESSO	
FRUIT	
HEADACHE	
HEART RATE	

```
I C O N I C C U P P A C A V
Z I S L L I P L A N T L O J
Z T R E T T I B E N E R G Y
U E E T E S S E N T R E L A
B R T N S N O I T C I D D A
K U T A P D F D Q L M B R S
W I I L R E T E A A O U I L
U D J U E T D B J W L L N E
H E G M S A R E C A E L K E
E C A I S L I A H R C E S P
A A W T O O N N E D U A V L
D F A S P C K S M H L V F A
A L K A L O I D I T E E R T
C R E P Y H P G C I H S U T
H C O C A C O L A W Q G I E
E E F F O C K O L A N U T P
```

Solution on Page 323

ARTIFACTS

BASEBALL

CAPITALIST

CHRISTIAN

CLASSICAL

CULTURES

DEMOCRACY

EDUCATION

EQUALITY

EUROPEAN

EXPRESSION

FOOTBALL

GLOBALISM

GREEKS

HERITAGE

HOLLYWOOD

LIFE

LITERATURE

MEDIEVAL

MODERN

MUSIC

PEOPLE

PHILOSOPHY

POWER

ROMANS

TECHNOLOGY

TELEVISION

TRADITION

Western Culture

```
L A V E I D E M N R E D O M
I N C E N A E P O R U E A E
L O U X T R A D I T I O N M
L I L P H I L O S O P H Y S
A T T R E Z A I I Y A Y F I
C A U E M O L I V C S T E L
I C R S R A P K E A T I B A
S U E S T A I L L R C L A B
S D S I X K T N E C A A S O
A E P O W E R U T O F U E L
L A S N A M O R R M I Q B G
C Y G O L O N H C E T E A R
I H O L L Y W O O D R Q L E
S C B C H R I S T I A N L E
U H E R I T A G E F I L N K
M L C Q L L A B T O O F N S
```

Solution on Page 323

PUZZLES • 157

AIRCRAFT	MODELS
AIRPLANE	MOTOR
ASSEMBLY	NONFLYING
BALSA WOOD	PAINT
BUILDING	PARTS
CHILDREN	PILOT
CONSTRUCT	PLASTIC
CONTROL	PROPELLERS
ELECTRIC	ROCKET
ENGINE	SCALE
EXPENSIVE	TAIL
FIBERGLASS	TOYS
FLIGHT	WINGS
FOAM	
FUSELAGE	
GLIDER	
HELICOPTER	
HOBBY	
JETS	
KITS	
MILITARY	
MINIATURE	

Model Aircraft

```
X J N O N F L Y I N G B O F
T S R E L L E P O R P K D E
G E Y E N E N A L P R I A L
Q L V O T G T E K C O R I E
B W I I T P I R O T O M R C
A P I D S C O N S T R U C T
L A I N E N T C E R M Y R R
S S A L G R E B I F O B A I
A S A V O S N P T L D B F C
W E I L O T E E X I E O T A
O M I N I A T U R E L H V T
O B U I L D I N G D S T E J
D L I A T O F U S E L A G E
Z Y R A T I L I M T N I A P
S C A L E M A O F L I G H T
K I T S T R A P L A S T I C
```

Solution on Page 323

BAKEWARE

BOWL

BRUSH

CLEANING

CLEAVER

COLANDER

COOKBOOK

COOKING

COPPER

CUTLERY

DRAWER

EATING

FLATWARE

FOOD

FORKS

FRYING PAN

GLASSWARE

GRATER

HOLDER

IRON

KNIVES

MORTAR

OVEN

PANS

PEELER

PLATE

POTS

PRESS

SIEVE

SILVERWARE

SKEWER

SPATULA

SPOONS

STOVE

STRAINER

TOOLS

WASH

Kitchen Utensils

```
D I U E V E I S E V I N K K
D R E D E E T M N X N E V O
O O A S O R E D N A L O C O
O N T W A A A R A T R O M B
F O I I E W Q W E V O T S K
P R N B A R E W E K S P E O
Y E G S S E R P I K A T C O
R T H B P V G N I N A E L C
E A B O W L G I S L R B E S
L R F R Y I N G P A N C A K
T G H T U S K G W H O T V R
U A L U T A P S S P C P E O
C K T O O L S U P J V D R F
F L A T W A R E R E L E E P
R M W C L B R S P O O N S N
A S F G M B U T H U K M X U
```

Solution on Page 323

ACROBATS

AIR

ATHLETE

BOUNCING

CIRCUS

COILED

DANGEROUS

DIVING

ELASTICITY

EXERCISE

FABRIC

FALLING

FLIGHT

FRAME

FREE

GRAVITY

GYMNASTICS

HIGH

INJURY

JUMPING

MAT

PADS

PLAY

REBOUND

RECREATION

ROUND

SAFETY NET

SCHOOL

SIT

SOMERSAULT

SPORTS

SPRINGS

STEEL

STRETCH

TAUT

TRAINING

TRAPEZE

TUMBLING

TWIST

Trampolines

```
E M S C O I L E D D R T P L
T A P F R E E N A D W H A O
R C O R B O U N C I N G D O
A R R A C O G H S Y T I S H
P O T M B E I T T A U L O C
E B S E R G N I L L A F M S
Z A R O H H C T E R T S E Y
E T U N O I T A E R C E R R
S S C I T S A N M Y G V S U
I Y I S A F E T Y N E T A J
C A A T U M B L I N G T U N
R L A S P R I N G S H M L I
E P G R A V I T Y L P A T E
X C I R B A F O E I N T I C
E S U C R I C T N D N U O R
L E E T S X E G N I V I D Q
```

Solution on Page 324

ACTIVITY	MEDICATION
BENEFITS	MENTAL
BODY	NUTRITION
BRAIN	ORAL
CARE	PHARMACY
CHILDREN	PHYSICAL
CLINIC	REST
DIET	RISK
DISEASE	SLEEP
EDUCATION	SMOKING
EXERCISE	STRESS
FITNESS	TREATMENT
FLU	WATER
FOOD	WEIGHT
GENETICS	WELLNESS
HEALTHY	
HYGIENE	
ILLNESS	
LEAN	
LIFESTYLE	
LIVING	
LONGEVITY	

```
G N I K O M S N I A R B Y X
P P U Q I L L N E S S O Y N
H L A T N E M U E S S D H O
Y C A M R A H P C I E Y E I
S H I E C I N I L C N M A T
I I F T A C T I V I T Y L A
C L O N G E V I T Y I B T C
A D W Y N I L B O E F R H I
L R A E N F E Y S N E M Y D
E E G G L N O I T A C U D E
S N N A E L C O T S P A S M
T W E F R R N M D T E A R R
R A I I E I E E L F E F M E
E T A X G N S A S S L I I A
S E E Z T Y R K I S S U D L
S R E S T O H D W E I G H T
```

Solution on Page 324

ACCESSORY

BASEBALL

BEANIE

BERET

BONNET

BOWLER

BRIM

CAPS

CLOTHING

COVERING

COWBOY HAT

CROWN

DERBY

DESIGN

FASHION

FEDORA

FELT

HARD HAT

HEAD

HELMET

HOOD

PANAMA

SHADE

SOMBRERO

STRAW HAT

STYLE

SUN

SWEATBAND

TOP HAT

TURBAN

VISOR

```
T O T E M L E H Z W M O D N
L P L Z D Y G U U U E I C B
O O E G N I R E V O C B R V
G S F T A H Y O B W O C H B
U T U R B A N Y S W Z E A O
C G J F T R D N L S P S R N
Z A Y D A D H E A D E E Z S
G U P E E H R P R B R C V T
S X C S W A G Y A B I U C R
F H R I S T N L M I Y K W A
T O O G E C L O T H I N G W
E O W N L F S E I N A E B H
R D N U Y T T O P H A T H A
E O A S T S T A V I S O R T
B W T H S V P A N A M A L U
O J P A S D F A R O D E F W
```

Solution on Page 324

BATHROOM

BEDROOMS

BUILDING

CABLE

CITY

COMPLEX

CONTRACT

CRAMPED

DWELLING

ELECTRIC

ELEVATOR

ENTRANCE

FLAT

FLOORS

HOME

HOUSING

KEYS

KITCHEN

LANDLORD

LAUNDRY

LEASE

LIVING

LOFT

NEIGHBOR

PARKING

PETS

RENTAL

SECURITY

SHARE

SINGLE

SMALL

SPACE

STAIRS

STORAGE

STUDIO

TENANTS

UTILITIES

WALKUP

WINDOWS

Apartment Living

```
J Y S P A C E X E L P M O C
T H R E E L E V A T O R I A
L F O Q M E G A R O T S D B
L H O U C O N T R A C T U L
A L L L S Y H H T C Y P T E
M I F S E I T I L I T U S I
S V D W Q A N I K R I K F C
R I E W B I S G C T R L L R
I N C K E Y S E L C U A A A
A G N I D L I U B E C W T M
T N A T R A L B N L E E N P
S I R C O U K I I E S F E E
H K T H O N L A N D L O R D
A R N E M D N E I G H B O R
R A E N S R S T N A N E T K
E P E T S Y W I N D O W S C
```

Solution on Page 324

AMUSEMENT

CARTOONS

COMEDY

CONTEXT

CULTURE

EMOTION

ENTERTAIN

FARCE

FUNNY

GAGS

HAPPY

HILARIOUS

HUMOR

HYPERBOLE

IMPROV

JOKES

LAUGHING

PUN

SARCASM

SATIRE

SENSE OF

SLAPSTICK

SMILE

SOCIAL

STAND UP

STORY

SURPRISE

TIMING

VERBAL

VISUAL

WIT

Humor Me

```
Z S K C I T S P A L S N L O
T U X S T O R Y N N U F A B
E R I T A S F T V P O N B H
V P O E M O T I O N I A R J
J R F A E A T W F A R C E L
G I O S S N O O T R A C V X
A S N H U M O R T O L I O E
G E L O B R E P Y H I V R G
S R U Y I T W L K V H I P U
T U C X N H S A R C A S M L
A T N E M E S U M A P U I Z
N L A I C O S G S Y P A S J
D U Y J U H O H E M Y L C G
U C O M E D Y I K C I P C F
P N X T X E T N O C U L F Z
V F T I M I N G J D T M E W
```

ANCIENT	OLD
ANTIQUING	PAST
ARTIFACT	PERIOD
AUCTION	PORCELAIN
BEAUTY	POTTERY
BUY	RARITY
CAR	ROADSHOW
CHAIR	RUGS
COLLECTION	SALE
CONDITION	SHOPPING
DEALER	TIME
DECOR	UNIQUE
DESIRABLE	UTILITY
ERA	VALUABLE
ESTATE	VICTORIAN
FURNITURE	VINTAGE
GEORGIAN	WOOD
HISTORICAL	
ITEMS	
LACE	
MUSEUM	
OBJECT	

```
H G N I P P O H S I T E M S
N E W D R A E G A T N I V D
R O O E R S R M U S E U M P
Y R O A O T U T I L I T Y O
U G D L A R N O I T C U A R
N I X E D A R E T F N C N C
I A D R S R N Y W O A O Z E
Q N V U H I S T O R I C A L
U T A T O T R U I T I O T A
E C L I W Y Z A C Q P N L I
S E U N R R D E B O U D W N
T J A R J O L B T L O I O R
A B B U I L T T U I E T N U
T O L F O A E C R Y C I C G
E D E C O R H E I C A O C S
S A L E Y Z P C X V L N V Q
```

Solution on Page 325

ABC

BASIC

BILL

BOX

BROADCAST

CBS

CHANNELS

CHARTER

CINEMAX

COAXIAL

COMCAST

COMEDY

DIGITAL

DISCOVERY

ESPN

EXPENSIVE

FCC

FEES

FOX

HBO

LINEUP

MOVIES

MSNBC

MTV

NETWORKS

NEWS

PACKAGES

PREMIUM

PROGRAMS

PROVIDER

REMOTE

SATELLITE

SERVICE

SHOWTIME

SPORTS

STATION

TBS

TELEVISION

TNT

VERIZON

```
M E T I L L E T A S B C L B
O L R E T R A H C W L A A C
V I Y L L I B R T N T S M B
I N F S A E D E P I I K U N
E E E W I V V D G C M R I S
S U E E X I Y I M T V O M M
E P S N A S D V S D B W E S
R R H O O N E O I I R T R E
V O O Z C E M R H S O E P T
I G W I I P O P L C A N S O
C R T R N X C E C O D O P M
E A I E E E N F B V C I O E
F M M V M N O W B E A T R R
A S E G A K C A P R S A T F
T B S H X O B H R Y T T S O
Z Z C O M C A S T N P S E X
```

ADMIRED	IDEA
ART	INNER
ATTRACTIVE	LOOKS
BEAUTIFUL	LOVE
BEHOLDER	MAGAZINES
CHARACTER	MEANING
CHARISMA	MODELS
CLASSIC	NATURE
COLOR	PERCEPTUAL
COMPLEXION	PERFECTION
CONCEPT	PERSON
CONTEST	PLEASURE
CULTURE	PRETTY
ELEGANCE	SKIN
FACE	SPA
FASHION	SYMMETRY
FEATURES	WOMEN
GIRL	YOUTH
GLAMOUR	
GRACE	
HEALTH	
HOT	

```
S K I N N E R U S A E L P H
F A C E M T D E R I M D A O
K G M Y R E R U T L U C G T
A O L A O U E Y P P C G I P
W M N A T U R E E E E O N R E
M A S A M T T C R R M I L C
O A E I E O R H F C P N U N
D F G M R O U A E E L A F O
E A M A L A S R C P E E I C
L Y E O Z H H A T T X M T L
S H C D I I R C I U I E U A
X C E O I G N T O A O V A S
E C N A G E L E N L N O E S
B E H O L D E R S P A L B I
G P R E T T Y T S E T N O C
L O O K S K H P E R S O N Q
```

Solution on Page 325

ASPIRIN

BIOMEDICAL

BODY

CLINICS

DIAGNOSIS

DISEASES

DRUGS

EMERGENCY

EXAM

FEVER

FLU

GENETICS

HEALING

HEALTHCARE

HOSPITALS

ILLNESS

INJURY

INSURANCE

LAB

MEDICATION

NECESSARY

NURSES

PAIN

PATHOLOGY

PEDIATRICS

PHARMACY

PHYSICIANS

PREVENTION

RELIEF

RESEARCH

SYMPTOM

TESTS

TREATMENT

```
H C R A E S E R E L I E F B
N N N O I T A C I D E M P A
U Y I P P F E V E R Y O R L
R L D R A H N P A R R T E T
S I F O I T Y C A V U P V I
E X A M B P H S K I J M E D
S S T C P T S O I S N Y N I
E Z L E L E N A L C I S T A
S M L A C I D E M O I B I G
A P E E T N N I M T G A O N
E H N R P I A I A T E Y N O
S D R U G S P R C T A S B S
I I L L N E S S U S R E T I
D H E A L I N G O S S I R S
O G E N E T I C S H N K C T
A P H A R M A C Y C R I T S
```

Solution on Page 326

ALIGNED

ASTRONOMY

ATMOSPHERE

BLOCK

CELESTIAL

CYCLE

DARKNESS

EARTH

ECLIPSE

EVENT

FULL MOON

HORIZON

NASA

NIGHT

OBSERVE

OMEN

ORBIT

PARTIAL

PASSES

PENUMBRAL

RARE

RAYS

REFRACTION

SCIENCE

SHADOW

SKY

SOLAR

SPACE

SUNLIGHT

TELESCOPE

TOTALITY

VIEWING

VISIBLE

Lunar Eclipse

```
E L B I S I V P T N H Z Z N
C A V K R J F V D H W Z E Y
N A S A Z Q Q Q R S G M V Z
E U P E S P I L C E O I E U
I B P O S S E N K R A D N H
C L L N E S U N L I G H T E
S A N O O M L L U F U R N P
R I O Z C Y C L E M A M T O
P T I I W K R A R E B A O C
A S T R O N O M Y R K R T S
S E C O D N D E N G I L A E
S L A H A B P A R T I A L L
E E R E H P S O M T A I I E
S C F A S V I E W I N G T T
K L E V R E S B O R R A Y S
Y O R B I T E C A P S K N L
```

ANIMATORS

AWARDS

BUG'S LIFE

CALIFORNIA

CARS

CARTOON

CGI

CHARACTERS

COMPANY

COMPUTER

DIGITAL

DISNEY

FAMILY

FEATURE

FILMS

FUN

GRAPHICS

HOLLYWOOD

LAMP

MONSTERS

MOVIES

NEMO

RELEASE

SHORTS

STEVE JOBS

STUDIO

SUCCESS

TECHNOLOGY

TOY STORY

WALL-E

```
R M O V I E S C I H P A R G
F D S S S E C C U S I E W S
R I G C A R T O O N U F A M
O N O L K Q Z F R M K I L L
I S T E V E J O B S P R L I
D R S F F C F E R U T A E F
U A R A N I M A T O R S N G
T C E Y L D L A W A R D S Y
S R T A R N O S F V J I S E
T E C H N O L O G Y U G R N
R L A M P N T P W U D I E S
O E R V P E D S Z Y B T T I
H A A F A M I L Y F L A S D
S S H T P O L Q A O M L N I
O E C O M P U T E R T Q O V
Z T E U H V T T F X M R M H
```

Solution on Page 326

ACES	KING
BETTING	MELD
BLUFF	MONEY
BRIDGE	OLD MAID
CANASTA	PINOCHLE
CARDS	PLAYERS
CASINO	PLAYING
CHEAT	POKER
CLUBS	QUEEN
CUT	RULES
DEALER	RUMMY
DECKS	SHUFFLE
DIAMONDS	SOLITAIRE
DRAW	SPADES
EUCHRE	SUITS
FAMILY	TRICK
GAMBLING	WAGER
GIN	WINNER
GO FISH	
HANDS	
HEARTS	
JOKERS	

Play a Card

```
M Y W J B U J O T R I C K T
E K J A U F R E G A W M S D
L A O M R H O N I S A C B J
D C K X E D I I N Y M M U R
E E E A L Y P I N O C H L E
C S R A A F A M I L Y T C L
K T S L E T M G S D N A H F
S I P D D O N G U M N T J F
L U L G N I L B M A G G L U
Q S A E T O R L S I I O F H
S U Y T W U M T W D B F R S
W D E F L K A A F R U I E P
K B R E R I A T I L O S K A
A N S A N N T D B D D H O D
T A E H C G G U C J Y S P E
L W I N N E R H C U E R G S
```

Solution on Page 326

ACCENT	IRONY
ALLEGORY	LIMERICK
ALLUSION	LYRIC
ANALOGY	METAPHOR
ANECDOTE	NARRATOR
AUTHOR	NOVELLA
BALLAD	PLOT
BOOKS	POETRY
CHARACTER	PROSE
CLIMAX	SATIRE
COMEDY	SETTING
CONFLICT	SIMILE
DIALOGUE	SONNET
DICTION	STANZA
DRAMA	STORY
EPIC	THESIS
ESSAY	TRAGEDY
FABLE	
GENRE	
GLOSSARY	
HYPERBOLE	
IMAGERY	

```
T O L P N K C I R E M I L E
N Y D E M O C Q U S K O O B
E R I T A S I G N I T T E S
C L I M A X O T C I R Y L R
C S I M I L E A C I P E P A
A I S E A L L U S I O N O L
N M V I R L A M A R D T E L
A A D G E N A N E C D O T E
L G F G L B E T V A P C R V
O E O A O O C G L R I O Y O
G R A S B A S L O L H D S N
Y Y U T R L A S F P E T O Y
A X T A E B E N A G O M N N
S N H N P R O T A R R A N O
S C O Z Y C E R Y S Y U E R
E Y R A H M T S I S E H T I
```

Solution on Page 327

ATTORNEY

BAIL

BILL

BOOKS

CASE

CIVIL

CONTRACTS

COURTROOM

CRIMINAL

DECISION

DEFENDANT

ECONOMICS

EVIDENCE

FINES

GAVEL

GUILTY

JAIL

JUDGES

JUDICIARY

JUSTICE

LAWYERS

LEGAL

ORDER

PLAINTIFF

PLEA

POLITICS

PRECEDENT

PRISON

REGULATION

RIGHTS

SCHOOL

SENTENCE

SHERIFF

SOCIETY

STATUTE

SUE

TORT

WITNESS

```
E C N E T N E S H E R I F F
D Y N V L E G A L U F M T R
X E B I G D E C I S I O N G
A N F D S T C A R T N O C S
E R L E T N E D E C E R P C
L O I N N J U D G E S T E H
P T V C T D E L U I K R T O
R T I E O L A S L V O U U O
I A C G R F A N A I O O T L
S S E N T I W N T C B C A A
O O A J U D I C I A R Y T W
N C A Y E C O N O M I C S Y
B I X L P L A I N T I F F E
L E C I T S U J R E D R O R
S T H G I R P O L I T I C S
P Y T L I U G A V E L I A B
```

Solution on Page 327

APPRENTICE

ARTISAN

BARBER

BLACKSMITH

BUILDER

BUSINESS

BUTCHER

CARPENTER

CHEF

COBBLER

CONTRACTOR

CRAFT

GUILD

IRONWORKER

JOURNEYMAN

KNOWLEDGE

LABORER

LOCKSMITH

MACHINIST

MANUAL

MECHANIC

PAINTER

PLUMBER

PROFESSION

ROOFER

SKILLED

STONEMASON

TOOLS

TRAINING

WATCHMAKER

```
C L O C K S M I T H C H E F
O H X A P P R E N T I C E C
B T O O L S S E N I S U B A
B B I E W A T C H M A K E R
L S R E T N I A P S R A G P
E T I R O N W O R K E R D E
R O T C A R T N O C D T E N
E N S I D K F A F A L I L T
B E I N L D A M E L I S W E
M M N A I V R Y S B U A O R
U A I H U O C E S L B N N E
L S H C G N I N I A R T K H
P O C E S R E R O B A L H C
A N A M E L A U N A M A F T
Y G M Z M R O O F E R K C U
D E L L I K S J R E B R A B
```

Solution on Page 327

ACTIVITY

AEROBICS

ATHLETIC

BICYCLE

BOXING

CARDIO

CIRCUIT

CYCLING

DIET

ELLIPTICAL

EQUIPMENT

FITNESS

GYM

HEALTHY

HEART RATE

HIKING

JUMP ROPE

LEG PRESS

LIFTING

MUSCLE

NUTRITION

OBESITY

PILATES

RUNNING

SPORTS

STRENGTH

STRETCHING

SWIMMING

TRAINING

TREADMILL

WALKING

WEIGHT

YOGA

```
H  E  A  L  T  H  Y  D  D  W  M  S  N  I
U  A  N  W  R  U  I  I  G  U  W  S  U  S
B  P  I  L  A  T  E  S  S  I  S  E  T  C
O  S  Z  J  I  T  L  C  M  T  E  R  R  I
X  D  S  U  N  Z  L  M  R  T  E  P  I  B
I  H  T  M  I  E  I  O  A  T  Q  G  T  O
N  D  R  P  N  N  P  R  C  R  U  E  I  R
G  O  E  R  G  S  T  H  T  E  I  L  O  E
N  I  N  O  V  R  I  I  A  P  O  N  A
I  D  G  P  A  N  C  K  V  D  M  B  L  E
K  R  T  E  G  I  A  I  I  M  E  E  I  L
L  A  H  M  R  D  L  N  T  I  N  S  F  C
A  C  Y  C  L  I  N  G  Y  L  T  I  T  Y
W  G  U  Y  P  B  A  T  H  L  E  T  I  C
F  I  T  N  E  S  S  J  A  G  O  Y  N  I
T  H  G  I  E  W  R  U  N  N  I  N  G  B
```

Solution on Page 327

ACADEMIC

AUTHORITY

CAMPAIGNS

CANDIDATES

CHANGE

CITIZEN

CORPORATE

CORRUPTION

DECISIONS

DEMOCRAT

ECONOMY

ELECTIONS

EXECUTIVE

FEDERAL

GOVERNMENT

GROUP

HOUSE

LAWS

MAJORITY

MILITARY

NATIONAL

PARLIAMENT

PLATFORM

POLITICIAN

POWER

PRESIDENT

PUBLIC

REVOLUTION

STATE

TAXES

VOTING

```
E A C A D E M I C I L B U P
V C L A W S N O I T C E L E
I H C Y N C A M P A I G N S
T A T M N O L A N O I T A N
U N N P I O I D S E X A T L
C G E P O L I T I C I A N A
E E M M B D I T U V P S H R
X P N E A U E T P L U C O E
E R R T U I G C A U O T U D
C E E A T A L T I R R V S E
O S V T H V F R P S Y R E F
N I O S O O W O A O I L O R
O D G T R G R O U P W O M C
M E I M I A C I T I Z E N Z
Y N P R T A R C O M E D R S
G T C E Y T I R O J A M U M
```

Solution on Page 328

AMP
ANALOG
BATTERY
BOARD
CAPACITORS
CHIP
CIRCUIT
COMPONENTS
COMPUTERS
CONDUCTOR
CONNECTION
CURRENT
DESIGN
DIAGRAM
DIGITAL
DIODES
ENGINEER
GROUND
INDUCTORS
INTEGRATED
LED
LOGIC

NEGATIVE
PARALLEL
POSITIVE
POWER
RESISTANCE
SCHEMATIC
SERIES
SIGNALS
SILICON
SUBSTRATE
TRANSISTOR
WIRES

Electronic Circuits

```
W I R E S C H E M A T I C S
L E L L A R A P S C Y A I L
A S N W W G X U O E P C G A
T H R Y R A B N D A R H O N
I Y I O R S N N C O E I L G
G D U E T E O I T D S P E I
I N W R C C T C P R I C V S
D O A T I O U T M A S I I P
P T I L R D M D A O T R T O
E O I S N P M P N B A C A S
N S G O L A N A O I N U G I
G E C U R R E N T N C I E T
I D S G D E T A R G E T N I
S O A D J R E E N I G N E V
E I L R O T S I S N A R T E
D D E L R C O M P U T E R S
```

Solution on Page 328

BACTERIA	MUTATIONS
BEHAVIOR	OFFSPRING
BIOLOGY	ORGANISMS
BREEDING	PARENTS
CELLS	RECESSIVE
CLONE	RNA
CODE	SCIENTISTS
DISEASE	SEQUENCING
DISORDER	STRUCTURE
DNA	STUDY
DOMINANT	TRAITS
EVOLUTION	VARIATION
FAMILY	VIRUSES
GENOTYPE	
HEIGHT	
HEREDITY	
HUMANS	
INHERITED	
LAB	
LIFE	
MEDICINE	
MOLECULAR	

Gene Study

```
Y T I D E R E H E G B A L R
G E V O L U T I O N K S N E
E V I S S E C E R I O L V D
N C R T T M O L E C U L A R
O O U B N S B M Y N I E C O
T D S A E Y I U S E N C O S
Y E E C R L O T G U H S R I
P V S T A I L A N Q E T G D
E R A E P M O T I E R R A O
N T O R N A G I R S I U N M
I R N I I F Y O P A T C I I
C A Q A V A G N S E E T S N
I I Y A X A T S F S D U M A
D T H G I E H I F I F R S N
E S N A M U H E O D C E A T
M G N I D E E R B N L I F E
```

Solution on Page 328

ARIZONA

BEVERAGE

BLACK

BREWED

CHERRY

COLD

COOL

DRINK

FLAVORED

GLASS

GREEN

HONEY

ICE CUBES

INSTANT

LIPTON

MINT

NESTEA

PEACH

RASPBERRY

RESTAURANT

SNAPPLE

SOUTHERN

SPOON

STEEP

STIR

SUGAR

SUMMER

SUN TEA

SWEET TEA

SWEETENER

TEA BAGS

TEA LEAVES

UNSWEET

WATER

Iced Tea

```
H C S D E R O V A L F D P L
O H B T K S E J K P E L M O
N E E L N N U N S W E E T O
E R V K O A I N E S T E A C
Y R E O S Q R R S T I R T I
N Y R H K W B U D W E S C S
O M A A T C E O A L Q E C X
O I G I S U A E L T C V W N
P N E H N P O L T U S A Q S
S T O U A S B S B T G E A U
S U B T P V T E E Z E L R B
C S M E P P S A R W L A I W
Q O A M L I B P N R C E Z A
O C L L E A L S N T Y T O T
H P A D G R E E N M J H N E
F Z L S U N T E A S U G A R
```

Solution on Page 328

AIR

ANIMALS

ATMOSPHERE

COAL

COPPER

DEPLETION

EARTH

ECOLOGY

ECOSYSTEMS

ENERGY

FISH

FORESTS

FOSSIL

FUEL

GAS

GOLD

GREEN

IRON

LAKES

LAND

LIMITED

MANAGEMENT

MINERALS

MINING

NATURE

OCEANS

PETROLEUM

PROTECTION

RAIN FOREST

RENEWABLE

RIVERS

ROCKS

SILVER

SOIL

SOLAR

SUNLIGHT

WATER

WIND

WOOD

Natural Resources

```
D E T I M I L Q G O L D U M
O C R B T S E R O F N I A R
C O P P E R E G P S D N A L
E L B A W E N E R E A R T H
I O E U N I T E F G H S I F
B G G C N R V S E P T N P A
N Y O I O I M M K S K A R Q
S A M L R S E D E C F T O S
L T E R I N Y R I A O U T O
A U H A T M O S P H E R E I
M W E G X F C Y T F Z E C L
I A N O I T E L P E D G T S
N T E W W L A K E S M A I O
A E R O M I N E R A L S O L
T R G O H S S U D N I W N A
V G Y D J F O S S I L V E R
```

Solution on Page 329

ACTING

APOLLO

AWARDS

BEST ACTOR

BIG

CAST AWAY

CELEBRITY

CHARACTER

COMEDIAN

DIRECTOR

DRAGNET

FAMOUS

FATHER

FILM

FORREST

FUNNY

GREEN MILE

GUMP

HOLLYWOOD

LOVE

MEG RYAN

MOVIES

OSCARS

PRODUCER

RICH

RITA

ROLE

SEATTLE

SPLASH

STAR

TALENT

TELEVISION

TERMINAL

TOY STORY

VOICE

WOODY

```
A G Q L O V E L T T A E S Y
C T U T S R A C S O T H A A
T W I M Y A P E Z R E S G R
I E B R P T R F S D R A W A
N I L O G R I E U Y M L O T
G L L E O R O R H N I P O S
C L C F V T E D B T N S D Y
O H I A A I M E U E A Y Y M
M O A T S M S O N C L F D D
E L O R N T O I V M E E I F
D L O I A E A U O I I R C I
I Y L C Z C L W S N E L P L
A W T H W P T A A C C S E M
N O D R A G N E T Y I I P A
R O T O Y S T O R Y O M N L
A D S N A Y R G E M V N M L
```

Solution on Page 329

ANIMAL	SMELL
BACON	SOW
BIG	STY
BREEDING	SUBSPECIES
DOMESTIC	SWINE
FARMING	TAIL
FEEDING	TRAINED
FERAL	TRUFFLES
FOOD	WILD BOAR
HAM	
HOGS	
HOUSE PET	
LITTER	
LIVESTOCK	
MEAT	
MINIATURE	
PETS	
PIGLETS	
PORK	
RUNT	
SAUSAGES	
SMART	

```
T  B  Z  B  S  A  U  S  A  G  E  S  T  Y
T  T  N  U  R  X  J  L  Z  N  F  E  G  K
S  A  V  T  P  T  T  M  I  I  I  L  D  L
D  E  N  I  A  R  T  C  C  D  L  F  L  S
R  M  I  N  I  A  T  U  R  E  K  F  R  R
E  A  P  C  N  R  H  N  M  E  Q  U  K  O
T  H  L  I  E  O  O  S  K  R  R  R  O  H
T  X  M  P  G  P  U  F  R  B  A  T  S  M
I  A  S  D  S  L  S  G  O  H  O  F  X  G
L  C  T  M  O  T  E  B  P  O  B  E  Q  N
U  H  E  V  A  M  P  T  U  E  D  R  S  I
Z  E  P  I  S  R  E  T  S  S  L  A  D  D
Y  R  L  K  C  O  T  S  E  V  I  L  Z  E
B  V  Q  N  U  L  W  D  T  S  W  I  N  E
F  N  A  P  N  B  I  G  N  I  M  R  A  F
M  S  M  X  Y  U  B  L  B  A  C  O  N  H
```

Solution on Page 329

ACCESS

CARE

CLINICS

COVERAGE

DENTISTRY

DIAGNOSIS

DISEASE

DRUGS

EXAM

FAMILY

HEALTH

HMO

HOME

HOSPITALS

ILLNESS

INDUSTRY

INSURANCE

LAB

MEDICINE

NURSING

OFFICE

PATIENT

PHARMACY

PHYSICIAN

POLITICAL

PRIVATE

PROCEDURES

PROVIDER

RESEARCH

RIGHTS

SERVICES

SPENDING

THERAPY

TREATMENT

UNIVERSAL

VACCINES

WHO

Health Provider

```
N S P R I V A T E C I F F O
U C H Q T N E I T A P H W D
R L A S R E V I N U D O H R
S I R R E D I V O R P M O U
I N M E A S E C I V R E S G
N I A S T H O S P I T A L S
G C C E M V L D I S E A S E
N S Y A E C N A R U S N I R
I T M R N M B Y B I A Z M U
D H A C T Y R T S I T N E D
N G X H L T H O C T W R D E
E I E I S E N I C C A V I C
P R M U R G S S E C C A C O
S A D A A Y S S E N L L I R
F N P I H T L A E H M O N P
I Y D P O L I T I C A L E W
```

Solution on Page 329

ADAKITE

ANDESITE

APLITE

BASANITE

CHALK

COAL

DACITE

DIAMOND

DIORITE

DOLOMITE

FLINT

FOSSIL

GABBRO

GNEISS

GRANITE

IGNEOUS

JADE

LIMESTONE

MAGMA

MINERALS

MUDSTONE

OBSIDIAN

PEBBLE

PHYLLITE

QUARTZITE

RHYOLITE

SANDSTONE

SCORIA

SEDIMENT

SHALE

SILTSTONE

SLATE

TONALITE

TUFF

TURBIDITE

VOLCANIC

```
T N I L F Q E T I N A R G J
N Z C O A L U L I S S O F A
E N O T S D N A S I D E E D
M K E T I C A D R L E T L E
I G N E O U S K S T I I A N
D I A M O N D C I S Z D H O
E M U D S T O N E T P I S T
S L A T E R A D V O E B T S
R C P R I S N O O N P R T E
G H H A A A B L L E E U O M
A A Y B O S A O C G T T N I
B L L O I P U M A N I M A L
B K L D L I M I N E R A L S
R M I I U I S T I I O G I L
O A T U F F T E C S I M T U
N E E E L B B E P S D A E H
```

Solution on Page 330

ACRYLIC

ALPACA

ANGORA

CASHMERE

CLOTHING

COTTON

CROCHETING

DENIM

DESIGN

DYES

FABRIC

FASHION

FELT

FIBERS

FLAX

HEMP

INDUSTRY

KNITTING

LINEN

LOOM

MATERIALS

MILL

NYLON

PATTERN

POLYESTER

RAYON

SATIN

SEWING

SILK

SPANDEX

SPINNING

SYNTHETIC

TAILORING

TEXTURE

THREAD

TWILL

WEAVING

WOOL

WOVEN

YARN

Textiles

```
C I R B A F E L T H E M P R
X R D Y E S P I N N I N G J
M A O A L P A C A N O N M S
I N L C G N I R O L I A T G
L G R F H L G T Y H T Y E N
L O X E Y E T N T E A J X I
K R O R T O T O R R C F T V
L A C W C T L I N E N A U A
I A I I H C A H N D G S R E
S L H R T L E P U G I H E W
L R E T S E Y L O P S I G M
H A E C A S H M E R E O N I
D L K B T Y R T S U D N I N
K O G N I T T I N K G P W E
W O V E N F G R A Y O N E D
C M J S X E D N A P S Y S J
```

Solution on Page 330

ADDRESS	MILITARY
AL GORE	MODEM
AOL	NETSCAPE
APPLE	NETWORKS
ARPANET	ONLINE
BRIDGES	PACKETS
CABLE	PHONE
CERN	PROTOCOL
COMPUTERS	RESEARCH
CONNECTION	ROUTER
DARPA	SYSTEM
DATA	TECHNOLOGY
DIGITAL	TELEGRAPH
E-MAIL	URL
GATEWAYS	WEB
GLOBAL	WWW
GOOGLE	
GOPHER	
HARDWARE	
INTERNET	
LINKS	
MAINFRAME	

Internet History

```
Q P B G L O D A R P A S H T
R Y H L E N I L N O O F H E
E L G O O G G H T N L S C N
T W E B N R I P A E Y S R A
U S Y A W E T A G T R E A P
O N G L W H A R D W A R E R
R E O U W P L G C O T D S A
U T L I I O G E E R I D E L
H S O S T G O L R K L A R I
E C N E W C R E N S I U M N
M A H G S R E T U P M O C K
O P C D M A I N F R A M E S
D E E I N T E R N E T F L L
E D T R L O C O T O R P P F
M C A B L E S T E K C A P S
U F L I A M E T S Y S S A H
```

Solution on Page 330

ACID-FREE	PEN
ART	PRINTING
BAGS	PULP
BOOKS	REAM
CARBON	RECYCLE
CELLULOSE	SANDPAPER
CUT	SHEET
ENVELOPE	STATIONERY
FIBER	THIN
GLOSSY	TISSUE
INK	TREE
JOURNAL	WALLPAPER
LETTERS	WEIGHT
LINES	WHITE
MONEY	WOOD
NEWSPAPER	WRAPPING
NOTEBOOK	WRITING
PACKAGING	
PAGES	
PAINTING	
PAPER MILL	
PAPYRUS	

```
K J S R E A M E J D O O W J
N O J T E N V E L O P E G T
I A O P A P E R M I L L N B
T M U B A T A F T Z P C I O
H O R Q E P I P I R R Y T O
G N N J S T Y O S B E C N K
I E A G O R O R N W E E I S
E Y L N L E E N U E E R A G
W S S I U U P R S R N P N
R S E G L S T F A S D Y N I
I O G A L S D R E P R W O P
T L A K E I K N A C L I B P
I G P C C T I P U L P L R A
N S G A B L E T T E R S A R
G N E P P R I N T I N G C W
N W H I T E E H S N I H T D
```

Solution on Page 330

ALEJANDRO

AMERICAN

ARTIST

AWARDS

CELEBRITY

CLOTHES

CONCERT

DANCING

ECCENTRIC

FASHION

HAIR

ICON

JUST DANCE

MADONNA

MEAT DRESS

MONSTER

MTV

MUSICIAN

OUTRAGEOUS

PAPARAZZI

PERFORMING

PIANO

POKER FACE

POP SINGER

POPULAR

ROCK MUSIC

ROMANCE

SONGWRITER

STAR

STYLE

TELEPHONE

THE FAME

VIDEOS

WOMAN

YOUNG

218

Lady Gaga

```
Z T S I T R A L U P O P R T
N A I C I S U M T V J Y O E
A O U T R A G E O U S O M M
M V I D E O S A S A E U A A
O P R H A I R T T M H N N F
W S E E S A D D Y E T G C E
Y C O G G A L R L R O N E H
T T E N N N F E E I L I C T
A R I C G I I S J C C C C E
M N E R A W M S T A R N E L
O A N C B F R R P N N A N E
N W A O N E R I O O O D T P
S A P N D O L E T F P C R H
T R Y A N A C E K E R Q I O
E D C I S U M K C O R E C N
R S U P I Z Z A R A P A P E
```

Solution on Page 331

ALGAE

BIOLOGY

BOTANIST

BRANCH

CELLS

CLASS

DISEASES

ECOLOGY

EVOLUTION

FLOWERS

FODDER

FUNGI

GARDENS

GENETICS

GRASS

GROWTH

HERBS

LATIN

LEAVES

MEDICINE

NATURE

NUTRITION

PLANT LIFE

POLLEN

RESEARCH

SCIENCE

SEEDS

SOIL

SPECIES

STEMS

STRUCTURE

STUDY

TAXONOMY

TISSUE

VEGETABLES

VEGETATION

WATER

Studying Plants

```
E N I C I D E M S F U N G I
S T U D Y B I O L O G Y E O
H T W O R G P S L A T I N E
Q J P P B O P V E W A T E R
J T M A L G A E C A N F T U
S S A L C A N G A O S S I T
D I E U E C N E I C S E C A
E N O I T I R T U N A L S N
E A H F L H U A L U R B R T
S T C Z C L S T D I G A E I
H O R N O M L I O S F T W S
E B A V E Y G O L O C E O S
R R E T A X O N O M Y G L U
B G S S T R U C T U R E F E
S R E D D O F Z L E A V E S
G A R D E N S E I C E P S I
```

Solution on Page 331

BAKERY

BAKING

BAKLAVA

BREAD

BUTTER

CAKES

CHEF

CHOCOLATE

COOKING

CREAM PUFF

CROISSANT

CRUST

CUSTARD

DANISH

DESSERT

DISH

DOUGHNUT

EGGS

FILLING

FLAKY

FLOUR

FOOD

FRENCH

ITALIAN

MILK

NAPOLEON

OVEN

PETIT FOUR

PIES

RESTAURANT

SCONE

SHORTENING

STRUDEL

SWEET

TARTS

TORTE

```
P I E S W C O V E N F T H L
H T U N H G U O D L D O O F
Y Y N A P O L E O N C R Y B
B I C A V X C U R O H T B A
U A A H S A R A O H S E R K
T S K F E S L K T D I T E E
T F E I F F I K N T N A A R
E F S L N N N O A R A L D Y
R U W L G G W L R B D O R S
S P E I H S I D U C I C A G
T M E N V A Y K A L F O T G
R A T G N I N E T R O H S E
A E F Z T R E S S E D C U N
T R U O F T I T E P G E C O
C C O K L E D U R T S U R C
H M I L K H C N E R F M S S
```

Solution on Page 331

ALBACORE

BIGEYE

BIOLOGY

BLUEFIN

BOATS

CANNED

CASSEROLE

CATCH

DIET

DOLPHINS

EAT

FILLET

FISHERIES

FISHING

FRESH

HELPER

IN OIL

IN WATER

LARGE

LOW FAT

MARINE

MELT

MERCURY

NETS

OCEAN

PINK

PROTEIN

RAW

RESTAURANT

SALMON

SALT WATER

SANDWICHES

SEAFOOD

STARKIST

SUSHI

SWIM

TIN

TUNA STEAK

YELLOWFIN

```
C A N N E D M W J K N I P K
E N L H C T A C Y F H H H J
E I M B A I F A I S B E U B
G E I F A R H S U L L N I T
R T W I E C H S U P A G I S
A O S S N E O E E E E N A S
L R H H R O F R C Y W N T T
Y P E I T I I O E A D N Y A
E R E N N S A L T W A T E R
N S U G W S M E I R E L L K
I E A C A T R C U I B E L I
R A W L R A H A D O K M O S
A F M K A E T S A N U T W T
M O H J S S M T E L L I F H
N O V N E T S Y G O L O I B
I D M R H I D O L P H I N S
```

Solution on Page 331

ADVENTURE	NALA
AFRICA	OUTLANDS
ANIMATION	PLAY
BROADWAY	PRINCE
CARTOON	PUMBAA
CHILDREN	RAFIKI
CLASSIC	SARABI
CUB	SCAR
DISNEY	SHENZI
FAMILY	SHOW
FATHER	SIMBA
FILM	SONGS
HAMLET	STAMPEDE
HYENAS	STORY
JUNGLE	THEATER
KINGDOM	TIMON
LIONS	WARTHOG
LOVE	ZAZU
MEERKAT	
MOVIE	
MUFASA	
MUSICAL	

The Lion King

```
E Z F R H Y E N A S P B U C
X D M B E C L E C N I R P I
T E L M A H C I T B L O H K
T G I N O I T A M I N A P I
A I F B S L Z A O A D D E F
M L M S A D K N F V F W L A
S L A O F R S I E X O A G R
A L Y N N E A N N H L Y N C
C A J G X N T S S G S E U C
I C G S O U T L A N D S J Y
R I W A R T H O G E V O L R
F S Y E N S I D P L Y O M O
A U I E I V O M E E R K A T
Z M X M S C A R T O O N I S
Z A Z U B T H E A T E R U T
M U F A S A A B M U P L A Y
```

Solution on Page 332

AUCTION

BIDDING

BRIDGE

CALL

CARD GAME

CHANCE

CLOCKWISE

CLUBS

COMPASS

CONTRACT

DEALING

DECLARER

DIAMONDS

DOUBLE

DUMMY

DUPLICATE

EAST

FOUR

HANDS

HEARTS

LEVEL

NORTH

PARTNERS

PLAYERS

RUBBER

SCORING

SKILL

SOUTH

SPADES

STRATEGY

SUITS

TABLE

TOURNAMENT

TRICKS

TRUMP SUIT

WEST

Contract Bridge

```
K E L B U O D U M M Y C V F
H T R O N S O U T H A N D S
F A T R I C K S C O R I N G
L C L O C K W I S E A A U K
L I Y S T I U S P M U R T S
A L G G U K R X O A C Z N B
C P I L E E U N H G T P E U
N U M K N T D R E D I D M L
C D S T S S A E A R O E A C
O Q R A E E W R R A N A N H
M A E B G D E A T C T L R A
P W Y L D A S L S S E I U N
A N A E I P T C A R T N O C
S K L W R S L E V E L G T E
S E P K B I D D I N G J M K
I Y M I R E B B B U R U O F D
```

Solution on Page 332

APARTMENTS

BOARD

BUILDING

BYLAWS

CITY

COMMUNITY

COMPLEX

CONDO

DWELLING

ELEVATOR

FACILITIES

FEES

FLAT

FLORIDA

HALLWAYS

HOMEOWNERS

HOUSING

LANDLORD

LEASE

LEGAL

LOFT

MORTGAGE

NEIGHBOR

OWNERSHIP

POOL

PROPERTY

RENTAL

RESIDENT

SELL

STRUCTURE

TENANT

TIME SHARE

TOWNHOUSE

UNITS

VIEW

Condominium

```
J L E G A L X E L P M O C H
U N I T S A T N A N E T W S
B T A R O T A V E L E N E E
E U A P F N R B G S C E I L
G Y I L A E L U E O O D V L
A N T L F R E I C P M I Z O
G H I I D Q T S S T M S W O
T A I L C I S M R O U E S P
R L D B L O N O E W N R N R
O L I I O E N G N N I A E O
M W C S R A W D W H T H I P
L A N D L O R D O O Y S G E
F Y E S A E L D E U L E H R
M S W A L Y B F M S O M B T
P I H S R E N W O E F I O Y
O V G N I S U O H B T T R S
```

Solution on Page 332

ACTION	MOMENTUM
ATOMS	NEWTONIAN
BODIES	PARTICLES
CALCULUS	PHYSICS
DIRECTION	POSITION
DYNAMICS	PROJECTILE
ENERGY	RELATIVITY
EQUATIONS	SPEED
FORCES	STUDY
GALAXIES	TECHNOLOGY
GALILEO	THEORY
GRAVITY	TIME
INERTIA	VELOCITY
KEPLER	WORK
KINETIC	
LAWS	
LIGHT	
LIQUIDS	
MACHINERY	
MASS	
MATH	
MECHANICS	

Classical Mechanics

```
L R Y P H Y S I C S C H B F
I W O R K D I R E C T I O N
Q I S N O I T A U Q E R D L
U S N G D E E P S L C Z I A
I E V A Y O H W I E H S E W
D L K L I G H T S V N C S S
S C E I R N C P C M O I Y C
H I P L Y E O A U S L N T I
A T L E J S L T S V O A I M
I R E O I C N A W I G H V A
T A R T U E M I T E Y C A N
R P I L M M A C H I N E R Y
E O U O X M A T H U V M G D
N S M O T A G A L A X I E S
I S T U D Y V E L O C I T Y
A C I T E N I K E N E R G Y
```

Solution on Page 332

ACORN

ALMONDS

BARLEY

BRAZIL NUT

BREADNUT

BUCKWHEAT

CASHEW

CEREALS

CHESTNUT

CHICKPEAS

COWPEAS

FLAX

FRUITS

GRAINS

HAZELNUT

HEMP

LEGUMES

LENTILS

MACADAMIA

MAIZE

MILLET

OATS

PEANUTS

PINE NUTS

PUMPKIN

QUINOA

RYE

SEEDS

SOYBEANS

SPELT

SUNFLOWER

WALNUT

WILD RICE

Edible Seeds

```
T S P E L T N V T E L L I M
I W D E T U N T S E H C A R
T E I E A T U N L A W C F E
E H B L E N T I L S A O R W
S S J R D S U S E D C W U O
N A B A A R Z T A Z F P I L
A C E H Z I M S N I E T F
E R F O C H I C K P E A S N
B S L R P A G L E I H S M U
Y N A N M P I N E N U T S
O I X H A Z E L N U T K D E
S A B U C K W H E A T N N M
N R T E Y E Q U I N O A S U
R G B S Y N I K P M U P D G
J K B C E R E A L S Q Q S E
T F D K S N B A R L E Y N L
```

Solution on Page 333

ALARM	MONTH
ANALOG	NOON
ASTRONOMY	PENDULUM
ATOMIC	QUARTZ
BATTERY	ROUND
BELL	SECONDS
BIG BEN	SETTING
CUCKOO	SOLAR
DAY	SUNDIAL
DECORATIVE	TICK
DIGITAL	TIMEPIECE
DISPLAY	TOWER
ELECTRIC	TRAVEL
FACE	WALL
HANDS	WATCHES
HOURGLASS	WIND
INSTRUMENT	YEAR
INVENTION	
LATE	
METRONOME	
MILITARY	
MINUTES	

Telling Time

```
Y H D I G I T A L E V A R T
D A N N P Y A L P S I D A O
N N U V B M D C L F U T L W
I D O E I O G I K E O K A E
W S R N G N O R C M B E R R
A E T T B O L T I O M S M A
L T I I E R A C T N U E S L
L U M O N T N E L O L C E O
R N E N S S A L G R U O H S
A I P X L A T E Z T D N C Z
E M I L I T A R Y E N D T F
Y R E T T A B A U M E S A N
C U C K O O D M C M P C W O
U N E V I T A R O C E D H O
L A I D N U S E T T I N G N
M O N T H S Q R U A R T Z
```

Solution on Page 333

BRAND

BUSINESS

CALIFORNIA

CAMERAS

CARTRIDGE

COMPETITOR

COMPUTERS

COPIER

DESKTOPS

DIGITAL

FAX

GARAGE

GLOBAL

HARDWARE

INKJET

KEYBOARD

LAPTOPS

MONITORS

NETWORKING

OFFICE

PALO ALTO

PAPER

PRINTERS

SALES

SCANNER

SERVERS

SOFTWARE

STORAGE

SUPPORT

TECHNOLOGY

TONER

```
N X D E S K T O P S T M G T
C O P I E R A W D R A H A R
J M O N I T O R S E S H R O
S J G N I K R O W T E N A P
R I N K J E T T D U R W G P
E E C P O L K I S P V B E U
T P N A A L G T A M E U G S
N E D O L I X E L O R S D T
I R L R T I A P E C S I I O
R A N A A N F M S I D N R R
P W L Y G O L O N H C E T A
A T D N A R B C R R D S R G
O F F I C E O Y I N E S A E
S O N S C A N N E R I P C B
M S A R E M A C D K S A A C
S P O T P A L A B O L G X P
```

Solution on Page 333

AQUIFERS	PURIFY
BATH	RAIN
BAYS	RUNOFF
BOATING	SEA
BOIL	SHOWER
BOTTLED	SKIING
BRIDGES	SPIGOT
BROOK	SPRINKLER
CLEAN	STAGNANT
CONSERVE	STEAM
CREEK	STREAM
CURRENT	TAP WATER
DAM	THIRST
DRINKING	TIDE
DROPS	TORRENT
FAUCET	WATERFALL
FISHING	WAVES
ICEBERGS	WELL
MINERAL	
POND	
POTABLE	
PUDDLE	

Here's Some Water

```
W R T L G N I I K S S S L M
C R E E K N M D N O P P L V
E P R W C O I I E K L I E W
D C U O O U W T N L O G W H
I R N D S H A A A E T O Y T
T F O M D P S F V O R T R A
W C F P W L R R B E B A O B
T T F A S E E I G H S I L B
G N T L T S F N N N E C T T
B E L A N P I I I K A E N S
R R W O A K U A H Z L B E R
I R C X N J Q R S T I E R I
D O M I G D A M I X O R R H
G T R N A E L C F F B G U T
E D P O T A B L E R Y S C V
S B A Y S T R E A M A E T S
```

Solution on Page 333

AIRTIGHT

BEANS

BOILING

CANNER

COOK

FACTORY

FISH

FOODS

FRESH

FRUITS

HOME

INDUSTRY

JARS

JELLY

LIDS

MASON JAR

MEAT

METAL

PACKAGING

PICK

PRESERVING

PRESSURE

PROCESSED

QUART

RING

SALT

SEALED

SHELF LIFE

SOUP

STORAGE

TIN

TOMATOES

TUNA

VACUUM

VEGETABLES

WATER

```
F Y C Z S B M B Q B P U O S
A O O N N H O M E T R A U Q
W U O G N I V R E S E R P G
R A K D L W T V H E S A I D
A I T I S T A E M V S J C F
A O N E T E L G D A U N K I
Q G Y G R F O E E C R O H S
S X P N L N D T L U E S N H
T H G I T R I A A U J A R S
I R F G N K W B E M E M N A
U E R A S D I L S B O A D R
R N E K C Y U E K M E T A L
F N S C D E S S E C O R P H
H A H A G F A C T O R Y F P
A C P P G L E G A R O T S G
F A N U T R J E L L Y L S U
```

Solution on Page 334

AUTOSAVE

BACKBOX

BANK

BONUS

BOUNCE

BUMPERS

BUTTONS

COIN

COMBO

DRAIN

FLIPPERS

FREE BALL

GAME

INLANE

JACKPOT

KICKER

LAUNCH

LIGHTS

MACHINE

MAGIC POST

MATCH

MODE

MULTIBALL

ORBIT

PLAYFIELD

PLUNGER

POINTS

POPPER

RAMPS

REPLAY

ROLLOVER

SLAM TILT

SLINGSHOT

SOUNDS

SPINNER

STOPPER

SWITCHES

TARGETS

Pinball

```
M U L T I B A L L D R A I N
I P L A Y F I E L D M M T P
L M A G I C P O S T P O A S
I T B R E V O L L O R D R X
G S E A U T O S A V E E G O
H T E M B O P D M S P S E B
T O R B A I L A T P P T T K
S P F O N C T O I M G N S C
E P R N K C H L L A I I N A
H E E U H S F I T R N O P B
C R K S G R E G N U L P O U
T E C N G E G A M E A U P T
I P I T O P K C A J N C P T
W L K O B M O C Y C E O E O
S A H C N U A L E F J I R N
Q Y J O R B I T S O U N D S
```

Solution on Page 334

ALITO

APPELLATE

APPOINTED

ARGUMENTS

BENCH

CASES

CHIEF

DECISION

DOCKET

FEDERAL

GINSBURG

GOVERNMENT

HIGH COURT

JUDGES

JUDICIARY

JURY

JUSTICES

KENNEDY

LAWYERS

LEGAL

MAJORITY

NINE

OPINION

PLAINTIFF

PRECEDENT

PRESIDENT

ROBERTS

RULINGS

SCALIA

SENATE

TENURE

THOMAS

TRIAL

WASHINGTON

```
S T L N S Y V Y O T I L A K
T N A O E R F D N B E N C H
N E I I C U E E R U N E T W
E D R S I J D N O I N I P O
M E T I T I E N F E I H C L
U C O C S T R E B O R G Y A
G E Y E U S A K Y I O I E W
R R R D J I L R Y V M N A Y
A P P E L L A T E S I S P E
S E S A C I I R G N H B P R
E C C X C R N N D I Y U O S
G S N I O M I T N O V R I A
D P D J E L E G A L C G N M
U U A N U E T A N E S K T O
J M T R U O C H G I H W E H
P L A I N T I F F Q M C D T
```

Solution on Page 334

ADVENTURE

ANCHOR

ANEMONE

ANIMATION

AQUARIUM

AUSTRALIA

BARRACUDA

CARTOON

CHILDREN

CHUM

COMEDY

CORAL

CRUSH

DARLA

DENTIST

DISNEY

DIVER

DORY

FATHER

FILM

FISH TANK

GILL

JELLYFISH

JOURNEY

LOST

MARLIN

MOVIE

OCEAN

PELICAN

PIXAR

REEF

SCHOOL

SEAGULL

SHARKS

SON

SWIMMING

SYDNEY

TURTLES

WATER

WHALE

Finding Nemo

```
E S O N O O T R A C O R A L
I S F E E R X Q Y E N D Y S
V K Y E N R U O J R J S E N
O R E H T A F E N O M E N A
M A B A R R A C U D A R S C
H H G I L L S C C I L U I I
Y S U K R D H U L N O T D L
P M U A N I M A T I O N L E
T I D R L A R U W L H E L P
S Y X D C T T I K R C V U J
I D R A S M U H C A S D G A
T E T U R T L E S M F A A N
N M A S S W I M M I N G E C
E O G M O J E L L Y F I S H
D C W H A L E M X N A E C O
F W A T E R Y R O D I V E R
```

Solution on Page 334

ARTIFACTS

BEHAVIOR

BIOLOGICAL

COUNTRIES

CULTURES

DIG

ECOLOGY

ETHNICITY

ETHNOLOGY

EVOLUTION

FAMILY

FOSSIL

GENEALOGY

GENETICS

GROUPS

HISTORY

HUMANITY

KINSHIP

LANGUAGES

LINGUISTIC

NATURE

ORIGINS

PEOPLE

PHILOSOPHY

PHYSICAL

RACE

RELIGION

RESEARCH

SCIENCE

SOCIOLOGY

STUDY

TOOLS

```
W Y G O L O C E C N E I C S
A G E N E T I C S P U O R G
I R E L I G I O N T O O L S
W S N N S E G A U G N A L A
C E O P E T H N I C I T Y K
A I I C H A C U L T U R E S
H R T P I I L A C I S Y H P
U T U S E O L O F A M I L Y
M N L B I O L O G I C A L D
A U O C O U P O S Y T H G U
N O V Q D I G L G O I R L T
I C E R U T A N E Y P R A S
T S N I G I R O I V A H E B
Y R A C E T H N O L O G Y P
R E S E A R C H I S T O R Y
D P I H S N I K F O S S I L
```

Solution on Page 335

ACTIVIST

ALMANAC

AMBASSADOR

AMERICAN

AUTHOR

BIFOCALS

COLONIES

DIPLOMAT

FATHER

FOUNDING

GENIUS

GOVERNMENT

INVENTIONS

JEFFERSON

KEY

KITE

LIBRARY

LIGHTNING

MONEY

NEWSPAPER

PATRIOT

POLITICS

POLYMATH

POSTMASTER

PRESIDENT

PRINTING

REVOLUTION

SATIRIST

SCIENTIST

STATESMAN

STOVE

```
F E V O T S C I E N T I S T
O B P G N I T N I R P G U A
U I R L M L S V S O A O I L
N F E I J I I E P H T V N M
D O S G A G R N O T R E E A
I C I H I D I T S U I R G N
N A D T D I T I T A O N A A
G L E N U P A O M D T M J C
P S N I Y L S N A W S E L I
O E T N R O O S S E F N M R
L I R G A M S V T F Y T I E
Y N E G R A E A E Y E N O M
M O H L B T T R R R K B C A
A L T M I S S C I T I L O P
T O A K L O A C T I V I S T
H C F B N E W S P A P E R W
```

Solution on Page 335

AWL

BALSA

BARK

BEAD

BENCH

BLADE

BOARD

BUILDING

BURL

CARVING

CHISEL

CROSSCUT

DADO

DOVETAIL

DRILL

FACE

FENCE

FLUTE

FRAME

GOUGE

GRAIN

GRIT

GROOVE

HAMMER

HARDWOOD

HINGE

JIGSAW

JOINT

KNOT

LUMBER

MITRE

MORTISE

PATTERN

RASP

ROUTER

SCRAPER

SOFTWOOD

SQUARE

VENEER

VISE

Woodworking

```
M O I B L H Z V E N E E R D
E T U L F P W T F D R A O B
B R I A U E M A R F L T U X
L R W D Q D C C S G E N T H
D L G E O E O F X G S I E A
R K E G U O G O E I I O R E
E C R R D E W R W N H J E Z
B A T A G L R T I D C G M I
M R I I B N N A F T R E M S
U V M N D R I M U O O A A L
L I A T E V O D O Q S H H I
R N R T I R E V L L S C M N
A G T D T B E K A I C N H B
S A H I N G E B N F U E Y N
P E S I V Q D A D O T B B H
R E P A R C S T D H T V D F
```

Solution on Page 335

AFRICA

ARABICA

AROMA

ARUSHA

BEANS

BLACK

BOURBON

BRAZIL

CAFFEINE

CAPPUCCINO

CATURRA

COLOMBIAN

DARK

DECAF

DRIP

ESPRESSO

ETHIOPIAN

FLAVOR

FRENCH

HAWAIIAN

INSTANT

JAMAICAN

JAVA

KENYA

KOPI LUWAK

LATTE

MOCHA

MUNDO NOVO

PACAMARA

PANAMA

PERU

ROASTED

ROBUSTA

SANTOS

STARBUCKS

SUMATRA

TIMOR

TYPICA

UGANDA

Coffee Varieties

```
T Y P B R A Z I L B L A C K
N D E C A F H W F R E N C H
A B S O T N A S T L J A V A
T A R O M A R R U T A C N R
S K C U B R A T S R M V O S
N N A I P O I H T E A M O V
I R P W S C A F F E I N E R
A O P W U O F A O T C A S O
D E U F M L R C V A A I P A
N R C T A O I I O Y N I R S
A O C M T M C P N N D A E T
G B I O R B A Y O E R W S E
U U N C A I P T D K I A S D
R S O H X A M A N A P H O A
E T T A L N B O U R B O N R
P A C I B A R A M A C A P K
```

Solution on Page 335

ACTION

ADVENTURE

AGENT

BOND GIRLS

BRITISH

CARS

CASINO

CHARACTER

CONNERY

DALTON

DR. NO

ENEMY

FILM

FLEMING

GADGETS

GOLDENEYE

GOLDFINGER

GUNS

HERO

MARTINI

MONEYPENNY

MOONRAKER

MOVIES

OCTOPUSSY

RUSSIA

SHAKEN

SPIES

VILLAINS

WOMEN

```
G I N I T R A M O V I E S C U
U I I D F L E M I N G I P N
N E K A H S I T I R B O I S
S C M L I F S V C A S J E N
G C H T H T N E G A L I S L
R O M O O N R A K E R R O G
L C S N E M O W S K I A O M
O E E Y E N E D L O G L H O
H W Q E R U T N E V D A F C
C A R S F U G B O F N N O T
Y O S N I A L L I V O O N O
M O N E Y P E N N Y B I I P
D N V N H R G A D G E T S U
K R V E E E Y Z J E M C A S
O D R M R R R U S S I A C S
A O D Y S S Y S G X R K D Y
```

Solution on Page 336

AMERICAN	MINNESOTA
APPAREL	MONEY
BOOKS	ONLINE
BULL'S EYE	PHARMACY
BUSINESS	PRODUCTS
CHAIN	RETAILER
CHEAP	SALES
CLEARANCE	SERVICE
CLOTHING	SHOPPING
CREDIT	STORES
DEALS	SUCCESS
DEPARTMENT	TOYS
DISCOUNT	VALUE
FOOD	VARIETY
FURNITURE	
GOODS	
GROCERY	
HEALTH	
HOUSEWARES	
JEWELRY	
LOGO	
MALL	

Target Corporation

```
W  K  Y  E  N  I  L  N  O  T  S  Y  O  T
S  S  E  C  C  U  S  H  I  Y  R  F  G  V
D  R  N  I  A  H  C  D  S  L  A  E  D  F
O  Y  S  V  I  M  E  Y  E  S  L  L  U  B
O  P  T  R  A  R  R  W  C  E  W  R  D  S
F  R  O  E  C  L  E  A  R  A  N  C  E  A
T  O  R  S  I  J  U  A  H  I  W  R  P  L
N  D  E  O  L  R  P  E  T  P  A  G  A  E
U  U  S  N  G  P  A  U  R  W  T  N  R  S
O  C  P  A  A  O  R  V  E  M  O  I  T  H
C  T  H  S  I  E  L  S  L  O  S  H  M  O
S  S  E  N  I  S  U  B  I  N  E  T  E  P
I  D  A  B  O  O  K  S  A  E  N  O  N  P
D  O  L  C  H  E  A  P  T  Y  N  L  T  I
R  O  T  U  L  L  A  M  E  R  I  C  A  N
M  G  H  Y  R  E  C  O  R  G  M  J  Z  G
```

Solution on Page 336

AIRCRAFT

ANT FARM

ASSEMBLY

BALLS

BARBIE

BLOCKS

BRATZ

DOLLS

FIGURES

FRISBEE

GAME

HOT WHEELS

HULA HOOP

JACKS

KEN

LEGO

MARBLES

NERF

POGO STICK

PUZZLE

STUFFED

TEDDY BEAR

TINKERTOY

TOY CARS

TRUCKS

WEBKINZ

WHISTLES

```
F N X D O L L S A A S N B Z
R I Y Z G D L N U I E Z F U
I S R Y D L W Y A R R N O G
S E R L A A N T F A R M N J
B L A B S E R U G I F S W P
E B E M T O Y C A R S T H V
E R B E R N K K Z C B U I K
L A Y S H E C N X R L F S F
Z M D S F W I X L A O F T S
Z D D A M K T F H F C E L K
U K E N B J S O X T K D E C
P S T E A B O M H D S V S U
N S W C R P G F L H E W C R
U P K A B Y O T R E K N I T
M S T T I C P O T J G T T N
B Z N F E M A G B F X O N I
```

Solution on Page 336

AIM

ALTITUDE

APOGEE

ASSEMBLY

BUILD

CONSTRUCT

DEPLOYMENT

EJECTION

ENGINES

ESTES

EXPLOSIVE

FINS

FIRE

FLIGHT

FLYING

FUN

GLIDE

HIGH POWER

HOBBY

IGNITION

KITS

LAUNCHER

MODEL

MOTORS

NOSE CONE

PAPER

PARACHUTE

PLASTIC

RECOVERY

ROCKETRY

SAFETY

SCALE

SHOOT

SKY

SMALL

SPACE

SPEED

STREAMER

THRUST

WOOD

Model Rocket

```
S P A C E R E H C N U A L P
N N P I N Y J S E T S E M J
F R O T K V E N S R O T O M
L E G S R E C O V E R Y D I
I D E A E T T I Y M O T E A
G U E L V C I T L A C E L Q
H T E P I U O I B E K F F I
T I N H S R N N M R E A I G
H T G S O T V G E T T S N F
R L I H L S S I S S R I S U
U A N O P N A C S D Y G T N
S S E O X O S M A L L L I H
T P S T E C W E F L I I K O
D E P L O Y M E N T E D U B
C E E T U H C A R A P E G B
P D O O W U F I R E P A P Y
```

Solution on Page 336

ACTIVITIES

ART

AUDITORIUM

BUILDING

BUSES

CAFETERIA

CHILDREN

CLASSROOMS

COLLEGE

COMPUTERS

CURRICULUM

EDUCATION

ELEMENTARY

ENGLISH

EXAM

GRADUATE

GYM

LEARNING

MATH

MIDDLE

MUSIC

PAPER

PEN

PLAYGROUND

PRESCHOOL

READING

SCIENCE

SECONDARY

STUDENTS

TEACHERS

TESTS

TEXTBOOKS

UNIVERSITY

```
Y T E X T B O O K S G Y M H
O Y E L S T U D E N T S U S
P T C O L L E G E M V C S I
E I N O I T A C U D E O I L
N S E H T A M L S S Y M C G
E R I C G S U A D E R P A N
R E C S N C P S Y I A U F E
D V S E I B L S R T D T E T
L I G R N U A R A I N E T E
I N R P R I Y O T V O R E A
H U A A A L G O N I C S R C
C T D P E D R M E T E T I H
E E U E L I O S M C S X A E
X S A R U N U G E A A M G R
A T T M Y G N E L D D I M S
M S E S U B D R E A D I N G
```

Solution on Page 337

BARK

BASEBALL

BOARDS

BOTTLE

BULLETIN

BUOYANT

CAP

CHAMPAGNE

CORK OAK

CORKSCREW

ELASTICITY

FLOATS

FLOORING

HANDLES

INDUSTRY

MATERIAL

NATURAL

PORTUGAL

RECYCLING

SEAL

STOPPER

SUBERIN

TILES

TISSUE

TREE

WALL

WINE

WOOD

```
H T N A Y O U B O A R D S R
Q N A T U R A L R F B A R K
R C L S S S T A O L F F E U
N H A N D L E S I B Z L P F
O A E L O L A G U T R O P I
F M S L L A W C D D D O O W
K P K A O K R O C T N R T T
V A B B E N O R X S E I S H
E G U E U W A K L C L N U G
U N L S S Y X S Y A S G B V
S E L A S T I C I T Y O E V
Q N E B I V L R S F T R R P
U L T W T I E E E T N P I U
M J I P N T E W L E Z L N L
F N N G A E C E I R R Z A R
E S B M V C L L T T L T I R
```

Solution on Page 337

BOOKS

BORROW

CATALOG

CDS

CHILDREN

CLASSES

COLLECTION

COMPUTERS

DICTIONARY

DVDS

EDUCATION

FINES

FREE

GOVERNMENT

HELP

INTERNET

KNOWLEDGE

LEARNING

LENDING

LIBRARIANS

LOAN

MAGAZINES

MEDIA

MOVIES

NONFICTION

NOVELS

OVERDUE

PUBLIC

READING

REFERENCES

RESEARCH

RESOURCES

SCHOOL

TABLE

TAPES

```
S G I N T E R N E T A P E S L
L D Y E L E A R N I N G X E
S O V R E S R E T U P M O C
R C A D A R M E D I A N K R
E A H N O N F I C T I O N U
A T S O R W O R R O B I O O
D A F E O N F I N E S T W S
I L V H E L P C T Y N A L E
N O I T C E L L O C A C E R
G G N I D N E L Q Y I U D M
C S E C N E R E F E R D G O
H C R A E S E R V I A E E V
P U B L I C H I L D R E N I
E U D R E V O F E L B A T E
B O O K S M A G A Z I N E S
N O V E L S E S S A L C D S
```

Solution on Page 337

APRON

BROOM

CARPET

CHILDCARE

CHILDREN

CHORES

CLEANING

CLOTHES

COOKING

DOMESTIC

DUSTING

FOOD

FURNITURE

GROCERIES

HOMEMAKER

HOUSEHOLD

HOUSEWORK

HUSBAND

IRONING

JOB

KITCHEN

LAUNDRY

LAWN

MANAGEMENT

MEALS

NUTRITION

PURCHASING

REPAIRS

SERVICES

SWEEPING

VACUUMING

WASHING

WIFE

WOMEN

```
R H G N I H S A W M E A L S
E U I T Y R D N U A L A W N
P S B R X J K I T C H E N S
A B K R O W E S U O H H O E
I A T B O N W O M E N O R C
R N G T S O I E P C U U P I
S D R N Y E M N A H T S A V
C C O E I A R R G I R E G R
L H C M K S P O N L I H N E
E I E E E E A R H D T O I S
A L R G T S U H O C I L P E
N D I A T F T O C A O D E H
I R E N W E F I W R N H E T
N E S A C G T K C E U K W O
G N I M U U C A V F B P S L
O D U S T I N G N I K O O C
```

Solution on Page 337

ACTIVIST

ALBUMS

APPLE

ARTIST

BAND

BASS

BEATLES

BRITISH

CELEBRITY

COMPOSER

CONCERTS

DIVORCE

ENGLAND

FAMOUS

GRAMMY

GUITAR

HARRISON

HEY JUDE

HISTORY

KNIGHTED

LENNON

LINDA

LIVERPOOL

LONDON

MUSICIAN

PAINTER

PERFORMER

PIANO

POP

RICH

RINGO

ROCK

SOLO

STAR

SUCCESSFUL

VEGETARIAN

WINGS

YESTERDAY

Paul McCartney

```
L O N D O N D N A L G N E L
G H G R A T I U G I R O C K
E S C N S T R E C N O C R H
Y T U I I Y S C L D I Y O S
M A T C R R A I S A T B V I
M R H R C O V D V I D A I T
A P V E G E T A R I A N D I
R E Y L R P S B L E T E A R
G R R P O M E S D B T C E B
S F O P K L E U F H U S A R
E O T A E B J F G U O M E Z
L R S C C Y A I C P L T S Y
T M I G E M N S M O N A I P
A E H H O K N O S I R R A H
E R M U S I C I A N S O L O
B L S G N I W P L E N N O N
```

Solution on Page 338

ADVERTISE

BOUTIQUE

BUSINESS

BUYERS

BUYING

CHECKOUT

CLOTHING

COMMERCE

CONSUMERS

CREDIT

CUSTOMERS

DELIVERY

DEPARTMENT

DISCOUNT

DISPLAYS

GOODS

ITEMS

KIOSK

MAIL

MALL

MANAGER

MARKETING

MONEY

OUTLETS

PRICING

PRODUCTS

PROFIT

PURCHASES

SALES

SELLING

SERVICE

SHOPPING

STORES

WHOLESALER

```
S E L L I N G N I P P O H S
P R O F I T N U O C S I D T
D U Y R E V I L E D E M B E
D E S E S A H C R U P O U L
R C P C U S T O M E R S Y T
S R M A K M O N E Y W W E U
G E A V R E L S C W H W R O
N M R Q S T C U D O R P S P
I M K V E I M M L Z H Y B R
Y O E S I T R E V D A O E I
U C T T S C S R N L U G W C
B R I O A A E S P T A K A I
L E N R L B U S I N E S S N
L D G E E R I Q A S D O O G
A I R S S D U M A I L I U L
M T A C H E C K O U T K Q S
```

Solution on Page 338

BATHTUB

BRASS

COPPER

COUPLING

DRAINAGE

DRINKING

EQUIPMENT

FITTINGS

FIXTURES

FLANGES

HEATERS

KITCHEN

LEAD PIPE

LINES

METERS

PIPING

PLASTIC

PLUMBER

PUMPS

SEPTIC

SEWAGE

SHOWER

SINKS

SKILL

SYSTEMS

TOILETS

TOOLS

TRAP

TUBING

VALVES

WASTE

WATER MAIN

WRENCH

Plumbing

```
D N S E N I L R U L G L J C
T N E M P I U Q E N L E F J
U I V G Q D R A I N A G E Q
B A L C A X D P W R E N C H
I M A O F P I R F S L O O T
N R V U I P B K I T C H E N
G E R P T R S U X N G G P F
K T E L T Q T S T S K I L L
Z A B I I E P U H C I S A
I W M N N G L M R E T Y N N
C R U G G A I U E A S A Q G
I O L Y S W O P S T R S B E
T K P T F E T N E E E K R S
P P I P E S B M D R T N A N
E C A W E T S A W S E I S E
S H O W E R T R A P M S S R
```

Solution on Page 338

AEROBICS

BARBELLS

BIKES

CARDIO

CLASSES

CYCLE

DUMBBELLS

ELLIPTICAL

EQUIPMENT

EXERCISE

FACILITY

FEES

FITNESS

GOLD'S GYM

GYMNASIUM

HEALTH

INSTRUCTOR

MACHINES

MEMBERSHIP

MUSCLE

PILATES

POOLS

SAUNA

SPORTS

STEAM

SWIMMING

TRAINERS

TRAINING

TREADMILLS

WEIGHTS

WELLNESS

WORKOUT

YMCA

YOGA

Health Club

```
G N I N I A R T U O K R O W
Y S E E F B A R B E L L S E
M E M B E R S H I P O O C F
N N W E L L N E S S E K I B
A I E O L G E L C S U M B T
S H I I N S T R U C T O R
I C G D P I L A T E S F R E
U A H R T M L C O L E F E A
M M T A I M E B Q C S F A D
M T S C C I B X L Y S A F M
A G O Y A W B S E C A C I I
E P O O L S M N P R L I T L
T N E M P I U Q E O C L N L
S V M Y G S D L O G R I E S
A N U A S R E N I A R T S N
D M H E A L T H A C M Y S E
```

Solution on Page 338

ARTIFICIAL

BEVERAGE

BOTTLED

BUBBLES

CAFFEINE

CALORIES

CANNED

CARBONATED

COKE

CORN SYRUP

CREAM SODA

DEPOSIT

DIET

DR PEPPER

DRINK

FANTA

FIZZY

FLAVORS

FOUNTAIN

GINGER ALE

GLASS

GRAPE

ICED TEA

JUICE

LEMONADE

LITER

ORANGE

PEPSI

REFRESHING

ROOT BEER

SEVEN UP

SODA POP

SPRITE

STRAW

SUGAR

SWEET

TAB

```
D H S U G A R E T I L S C V
O R A N G E I C E D T E A P
W P U R Y S N R O C G P C U
S E B Y T G P E X A P O T N
R P O T E I D R R N K P I E
O S T R R N F E I E I A S V
V I T E E G V I N T T D O E
A Y L P E E P A C N E O P S
L Z E P B R U D U I A S E E
F Z D E T A N O B R A C D L
A I R P O L F S S S A L G B
N F I R O E W M J U I C E B
T G N D R E D A N O M E L U
A H K R E F R E S H I N G B
W A R T S E I R O L A C B A
E N I E F F A C E P A R G T
```

Solution on Page 339

AMPLIFIER

ANALOG

APPLIANCES

BIT

BOARD

CAPACITORS

CIRCUIT

COMPLEX

COMPONENTS

COMPUTERS

CONDUCTOR

CORE

DESIGN

DEVICE

DIGITAL

ELECTRONIC

ELEMENTS

ENGINEER

HARDWARE

MEMORY

MICROCHIP

MODERN

PASSIVE

POWER

PROCESSOR

RAM

RESISTOR

SILICON

SOLDER

SUBSTRATE

TECHNOLOGY

TRANSISTOR

VLSI

WIRE

```
R  J  M  A  R  O  T  S  I  S  N  A  R  T
O  R  E  D  L  O  S  C  O  M  P  L  E  X
T  I  U  C  R  I  C  S  W  P  B  R  J  P
C  E  R  O  C  A  M  P  L  I  F  I  E  R
U  E  C  A  P  A  C  I  T  O  R  S  T  O
D  L  L  H  A  N  A  L  O  G  E  T  A  C
N  E  A  E  N  N  W  R  D  M  E  N  R  E
O  M  V  T  C  O  O  O  E  E  N  E  T  S
C  E  L  E  I  T  L  W  S  M  I  N  S  S
I  N  S  A  S  G  R  O  I  O  G  O  B  O
L  T  I  I  Z  A  I  O  G  R  N  P  U  R
I  S  S  B  O  A  R  D  N  Y  E  M  S  E
S  E  P  I  H  C  O  R  C  I  M  O  K  W
R  N  S  R  E  T  U  P  M  O  C  C  T  O
H  A  R  D  W  A  R  E  V  I  S  S  A  P
C  Q  E  C  I  V  E  D  N  R  E  D  O  M
```

Solution on Page 339

APPRENTICE

APRON

BAKE

BURN

CATERING

COOKING

CREATE

CUISINE

CULINARY

DESSERT

DINNER

DISHES

EXECUTIVE

FOOD

FRENCH

GRILL

HAT

HEAD

HOTELS

KITCHENS

KNIVES

LINE COOK

MEAT

MENU

ORDER

OVEN

PANTRY

PASTRY

PLATING

POT

PREPARE

PROFESSION

RESTAURANT

SALAD

SKILLED

SOUS

SPECIAL

TRAINING

UNIFORM

```
S P E C I A L X H G S O U S
Y R T N A P R O N N Y F K G
Y R T S A P E L L I R G B T
S O R D E R N V E K A B O M
K I T C H E N S E O N P V M
I T R F A N I R V O I W E T
L E E L T T D E I C L N N M
L E S I U I Y S T B U R N R
E R S N N C S T U G C G P C
D A E E I E E A C N R C L S
I P D C F F V U E I E U A M
S E L O O R I R X N A I T B
H R R O R E N A E I T S I O
E P D K M N K N K A E I N E
S A L A D C A T E R I N G H
S L E T O H M E A T H E A D
```

Solution on Page 339

ABDOMEN

ANIMAL

ANTENNAE

BRIGHT

BUTTERFLY

CHANGE

CHRYSALIS

DAMAGE

EAT

EGGS

EYES

FUZZY

GARDEN

GREEN

HAIRY

HERBIVORE

INCHWORMS

INSECT

LARVAL

LEAVES

MONARCH

MOTHS

PESTS

PLANTS

PUPA

SEGMENTED

SILK

SLIDING

SMALL

SPECIES

SPRING

STAGE

SUMMER

TREE

TUBULAR

YELLOW

Caterpillar

```
W D E T N E M G E S L T K T
O N E E R G F B R P A G L R
L E A V E S R A O R R N I E
L P T E Y I R Y V I V I S E
E F D C G L A M I N A D P K
Y U S H E A F S B G L I U Y
Q Z T A S S T R R O N L P P
P Z N I U Y N S E C O S A D
E Y A R M R E I H T P N A N
S J L Y M H H W U E T M V E
T E P W E C O B C E A U A G
S Y Q G R R U I N G R T B N
H E G A M L E N E M O D B A
T S N S A S A L L A M S S H
O O H R N E D R A G W X H C
M U O W N T B Q J I I V B H
```

Solution on Page 339

AFRICA

ANIMAL

BANANA

BONOBO

BRAIN

CAPTIVITY

CHIMP

CIRCUS

CLIMBING

COMMUNITY

CONGO

EVOLUTION

FAMILY

FOREST

FUNNY

GOODALL

GORILLA

GREAT APE

HABITAT

HANG

LONG ARMS

MAMMAL

MONKEY

NO TAIL

OMNIVOROUS

ORANGUTAN

PET

PRIMATE

RESEARCH

SCIENCE

SOCIAL

SPACE

STRENGTH

STRONG

STUDY

TOOLS

WALK

WILD

ZOO

Chimpanzees

```
A S N T F B G C I R C U S V
B O O E O O L S P A C E C T
R C A P R N A U Z O O A I A
A I F O E O M O P S P W E T
I A R R S B I R R T M I N I
N L I A T O N O I R I L C B
S U C N C M A V M O H D E A
T V A G S O I I A N C V L H
U S G U R T M N T G O L A Y
D T N T Y E G M E L I N F E
Y R I A M N A O U R A Y A K
N E B N A M O T O N W B M N
N N M H M G I G A D I A I O
U G I A N O G B J P A T L M
F T L O N G A R M S E L Y K
Z H C R A E S E R T O O L S
```

Solution on Page 340

ALARM

ANALOG

BAND

BATTERY

BRACELET

CASIO

CHAIN

CITIZEN

CLOCK

DATE

DIAMOND

DIGITAL

ELECTRONIC

EXPENSIVE

FASHION

GOLD

HOUR HAND

JEWELS

MECHANICAL

METAL

MINUTES

NUMBERS

PLASTIC

POCKET

QUARTZ

REPAIR

SECONDS

SEIKO

SILVER

SPRING

STOPWATCH

STRAP

SWATCH

SWISS

TIMEPIECE

WATERPROOF

WRISTWATCH

Watch It

```
S O E X P E N S I V E L Z D
W K C F G O L A N A L M T Y
I I E O O C I T I Z E N R J
S E I O I S A C P C C E A E
S S P R I N G O H H T M U W
W K E P L G C A A T R G Q E
A C M R K K N I A A O T H L
T O I E E I N B L L N E O S
C L T T C E T A D D I L U R
H C T A W P O T S I C E R I
S I L W R I S T W A T C H A
I T A S E T U N I M A A A P
L S T D F A S H I O N R N E
V A E S R E B M U N W B D R
E L M L A T I G I D N A B Q
R P A R T S D N O C E S U B
```

Solution on Page 340

ASH	KNOTS
BAMBOO	LOG
BARK	LUMBER
BIRCH	MAHOGANY
BOARDS	MAPLE
BUILD	OAK
BURN	PAINT
CARVING	PAPER
CEDAR	PINE
CHERRY	PLYWOOD
CHOP	SAND
CUT	SAWDUST
ELM	SOFTWOOD
FIBROUS	STAIN
FINISH	TABLE
FLOORING	TIMBER
FOREST	TREES
FUEL	WALNUT
GRAIN	
HARDWOOD	
HICKORY	
HOUSES	

```
L D X E L P A M F P A P E R
V T D D E L M S U I A X Z Y
A I M S U Y R R E H C I E H
M M H M O W A G L S T O N K
M B B A F O R E S T U Y I T
K E K Y R O K C I H N O P E
R R S C E D A R D A S F H R
A T U N L A W T G L L A N Y
B D O O W T F O S O I C O L
S T R E E S H H O U G U O G
T A B L E A O R H D D T B C
A Q I O M P I S A N D W M L
I F F G G N I V R A C P A X
N I A R G N K S D R A O B S
N R U B I R C H Q B L H G F
G G R F L F M N C N S C E G
```

Solution on Page 340

ABALONE

ALGAE

BACTERIA

BALEEN

CAVIAR

CETACEAN

CLAMS

COPEPODS

CORAL

CRAB

DETRITUS

DIATOMS

DIVER

DOLPHIN

EEL

EGGS

HUMPBACK

KRILL

MARLIN

MOLLUSK

NARWHAL

NAUTILUS

OCTOPUS

OYSTERS

PORPOISE

SALMON

SCALLOPS

SEA LIONS

SEA OTTER

SEAWEED

SHARK

SHRIMP

SPONGES

SQUID

STARFISH

STURGEON

SUBMARINE

SWORDFISH

TUNA

```
D I U Q S F G C R A B S N E
A D E E W A E S I O P R O P
S E A O T T E R S H M A M K
E E N I R A M B U S I I L R
G G U L L A A A P I R V A A
N G T I R C K B O F H A S H
O S O L T E C A T D S C N S
P N I E C T A L C R O L O M
S N R O K A B O O O Y A E O
C I R R L C P N L W S H G L
A A I G L E M E G S T W R L
L L A A P A U D I V E R U U
L E M O C N H S I F R A T S
O S D E T R I T U S S N S K
P S U L I T U A N E E L A B
S M O T A I D O L P H I N N
```

Solution on Page 340

AGENTS

APARTMENTS

APPRAISAL

BANK

BROKER

BUILDING

BUSINESS

BUYING

CLOSING

COMMERCIAL

COMMON LAW

CONTRACT

DUPLEX

EQUITY

FOR SALE

HOMES

HOUSING

INTEREST

INVESTMENT

LAND

LEASE

LICENSE

LISTING

LOANS

LOCATION

MARKET

MORTGAGES

OFFER

OWNERS

PRICE

PROPERTY

REALTOR

RENT

SALES

SELLING

TAXES

VALUE

VIEW

YARD

```
R E E S N E C I L B V G H L
P Q E Z L O C A T I O N A I
B U S I N E S S E B V I G S
P I A A W I R W K U A S E T
O T E P A S E C R I L U N I
S Y L R L E N O A L U O T N
T T P O N X W M M D E H S G
C P N P O A O M K I C N E N
A T N E M T S E V N I Y R I
R I K R M M O R T G A G E S
T O T T O T E C I R P B T O
N N T Y C J R I D H E S N L
O B E L S E L A S R O F I C
C C A R A X E L P U D M F G
G N I L L E S S N A O L E O
D B R O K E R G N I Y U B S
```

ANIMALS

ARTIFACTS

AUTOGRAPHS

BOOKS

BOTTLES

BUTTONS

CANS

CDS

CHINA

COINS

CURRENCY

DISNEY

DOLLS

FIGURINES

FILMS

FURNITURE

GLASS

GUNS

HATS

JEWELRY

KEYS

MAGAZINES

MAPS

MODEL CARS

MUSIC

NEWSPAPERS

PLATES

POST CARDS

POTTERY

RECORDS

ROCKS

SEASHELLS

STAMPS

TEAPOTS

THIMBLES

TOYS

TRAINS

WINE

```
Q Y D Y E S E N I R U G I F
B R O U H A T S S K O O B J
S E L T T O B C L A N I H C
D T L E N S D R A C T S O P
R T S A E H L W M F B N C A
O O S P W P M I I I O U O
C P A O S A J N N L C T R E
E L L T P R T E A M P T R M
R A G S A G A R W S S U E A
O T Y P P O Y C A E T B N G
C E T M E T J E L I L R C A
K S O A R U C B N E N R Y Z
S N Y T S A M R S S D S Y I
N I S S N I U V F D I O L N
U O E S H F M U S I C D M E
G C X T O S E A S H E L L S
```

Solution on Page 341

Answers

Sewing Circle

Penny

Dairy

Trading Cards

Financial Investment

Radio Broadcasting

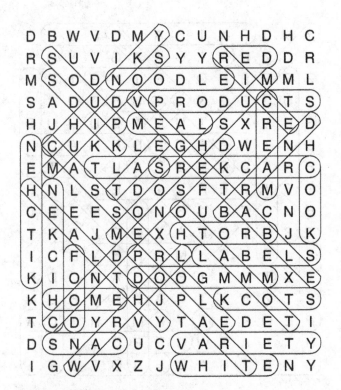

Campbell's Soup

Paleontology

Furniture Types

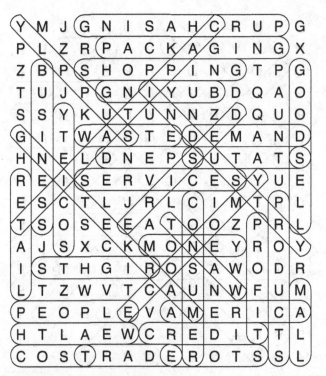

Construction

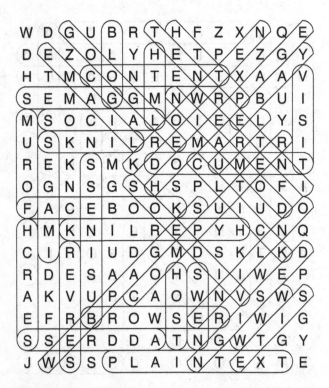

On the Web

Consumerism

Physics Class

Home Appliance

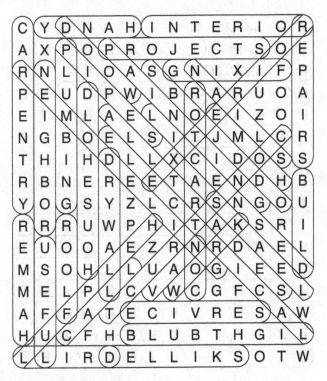

Handyman

Siblings

```
W I M O R T A R O L O C A Y
K R O O F S E G F L A T W H
U L K O S S R E W O H S E A
Q O D Q U A R R Y W A T E R
K G R E N G I S E D A T F D
J I U I C D G C S L I C G M
B A T H R O O M S H H E L Q
S E N C P F R O W A N R A P
Q C T I H L P A W O W A Z S
U G T R A E A A T N E M E C
A M E T A L N S T I L I D R
R G N I L I E C T T V C J X
E L B R A M J C F I E E F Z
J U L F I T U O R G C R O T
W A L L S C F L O O R I N G
Y N F G S L J C N F P B Y S
```

Tiles

```
A T H L E T I C U R L I N G
S C O R E Q S O F T B A L L
R A M A T E U R U N N I N G
E Z Y N O I T I R T U N O G
Y B G U R B N G P E M A G N
A L N Y T R O P S M A E T I
L I T M L I Y L P E G L L L
P E N E F N T L L O T N H W
H K I N E I A M A L H I T O
Y C A N V E S B I I M Y B
S I R I E D R X T T C M R O
I R T S I R C V E I S I E X
C C A C U V E X K C C W H I
A B I L A C R O S S E S C N
L N E F O O T B A L L L R G
E S N S C I T A B O R E A T
```

Sporting Chance

```
L K C I T S N O N Q R Z S A
A A F E N O C I L I S S L Q
T P D P I E P A N C A U I C
E P C L X R O K H U M X S I
M C A K E P A N C I Q S N M
J V S E R A W E N O T S E A
Z N S Q Y X P U A O T Q T R
Y A E C P A M E P S E S U E
H P R V N Z K B F S F E B C
T G O S O O I U A A L L B O
T N L K R H T N O L O D O P
W I E I I R C D L G N D W P
K Y F L T F H T O B W I L E
A R R L S M E P U O M R S R
T F K E A F N A K D F G D T
P P S T C K G N I T S A O R
```

Cookware

```
S E G A E N I L D O O L B P
U U T P K S O F T W A R E R
P A S T N O I T A C O L T E
D D N N R O B E I M B F Y L
H C R A E S E R E A R A R A
B Y T E I C O S N R O M D T
A S N O I T I D A R T I L I
P Y R T S E C N A I H L A V
T R S I S Y L A N A E I R E
I A H F J P E D I G R E E S
S R N C H I L D R E N S H T
M B S G N I L B I S E M A N
N I S U O C P S U R N A M E
E L P O E P P S D R O C E R
K X R E H T A F B I R T H A
M O T H E R K I N S H I P P
```

Family Tree

Whoopi Goldberg

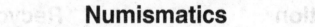

Numismatics

Journalism

Biology

Extinction

Recyclable

Elvis

Speaking of Horses

310

Shed

```
X W G M S T O R A G E L O P
S P A C E S R F A N X L L N
E P A I N T B R N I V A O Y
D R A Y K C A B G T S M C S
I E E L Q G R L N T N S K L
S T R W E G N U I O M S E L
T L U O O E N C N P H E D A
U E T R M M T I E O O I K W
O H C K J R N S D U B L H T
Y S U S E A E W R L B P U O
M K R H S F M O A V I P K O
T O T O U Y P O G L E U I L
E O S P O I I D K C S S B S
G H C E H D U E V I N Y L P
L J P E P H Q N F O O R T E
B B I K E S E V L E H S L M
```

The Scientific Method

```
S T L U S E R E S E A R C H
E V I T C E J B O P T U H T
G N I N O S A E R H A S E I
D P R O C E D U R E D C M N
E M P I R I C A L N N I I Q
L O R T N O C R S O M E S U
W S E E X P E R I M E N T I
O E D J R T Q S S E A T R R
N U I L E L U L E N S I Y Y
K Q C S A L E A H A U S G E
D I T B C O S N T L R T O V
O N I N T G T A O E A S L R
H H O W I I L P D B T O E S
T C N P O C O Y Y O L E I B
E E B S N X N Z H M E P B B
M T H E O R I E S J F S Y O
```

Get Some Sun

```
C G N I M M I W S A L O N H
O G N P T A H T B O O T H S
P O V I T A M I N D T C U T
P H K K H E A L T H L E V B
E S H N O T O Y G S E T R I
R K R E T M A I T S S O A K
T T O E G K L B T U N R Y I
O R L R B N A O N Z A P S N
N E O C U G B G E U R E B I
E M C S I O L R X Q S R B P
L M U N E A R I P A L E K W
K U G U S R A N O I T O L P
N I S P F J S S Y C K L K
I N E N R U B N U S B W R F
R S S E L K C E R F Q A U P
W L G N I X A L E R D R B S
```

Cookies

```
R H G U O D N U O R L F E Y
U E K E G I R L S C O U T Q
O K C H I P S C H E F H S X
L C W I C H O C O L A T E L
F R U T P E E P R J E I I Z
Q B U T T E R B T Y G U N N
S W E E T E O R B N G C W X
O P M X S E E V R H S S O U
F O F S A S R J E T P I R S
R R E T S N O M A N I B U L
C D A E R S A F D R C A S A
A L D E T I T F O S E K N A
F K M L C R M I N I S I A R
Q T G I N G E R U T J N C H
V A N I L L A A U R L G K O
B G T H H K L N T C F B X A
```

Programming Languages

Alternative Medicine

Intoxicating

Earth Science

312

Bank Terms

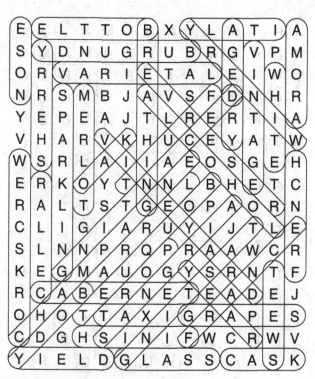

Galileo Galilei

Latin

Speaking of Wine

Domesticated Animals

Emotional

String Instruments

Entertainment

314

Child Development

Stamp It

Side Dish

iPad

Jellyfish

```
T O X I C F L O A T I N G T
G A D U M B R E L L A M S F
O B L O O M S I N A G R O O
D E R F O P G N I M M I W S
S A I R E F S F N A T U R E
W C G E L A T I N O U S C I
A H D S M U I R A U Q A U L
R P E H C R N S O R A O B L
M A A W L E G T Z A N Z O E
S I D A E L I A O G I O Z J
G N L T A I N I H E M S O N
O F Y E R A G D P N A U A O
C U R R E N T S Y I L D H S
E L U F R O L O C V A E S I
A O Z O R U A T S A F M I O
N X S E L C A T N E T S F P
```

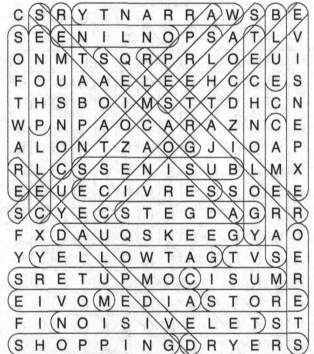

Computer Software

```
I P U T O O L S Y S T E M E
N F R E E W A R E M L I S C
S S C O M P U T E R D E W I
T J E C C W P M A D M I T F
A F B C O E O V L A N U U F
L I O R A R D E G D S N E O
L R D S Y F W U O E C D R T
W M A S O A R W R T D A A J
V W P S R R S E I E I O W A
D A R E D O C O T N S L E V
R R O N G A N I H N K N R A
I E G I P P C A M G I W A P
V J R S M P O H S O T O H P
E G A U G N A L A T A D S L
R D M B H A R D W A R E M E
S U S Y N T A X U N I L Q L
```

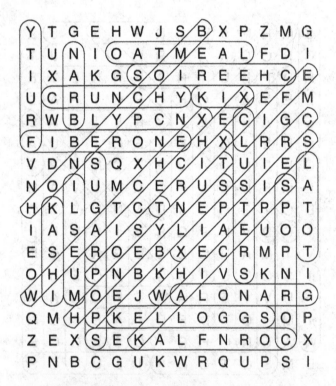

Breakfast Cereals

```
Y T G E H W J S B X P Z M G
T U N I O A T M E A L F D I
I X A K G S O I R E E H C E
U C R U N C H Y K I X E F M
R W B L Y P C N X E C I G C
F I B E R O N E H X L R R S
V D N S Q X H C I T U I E L
N O I U M C E R U S S I S A
H K L G T C T N E P T P P T
I A S A I S Y L I A E U O O
E S E R O E B X E C R M P T
O H U P N B K H I V S K N I
W I M O E J W A L O N A R G
Q M H P K E L L O G G S O P
Z E X S E K A L F N R O C X
P N B C G U K W R Q U P S I
```

Best Buy

```
C S R Y T N A R R A W S B E
S E E N I L N O P S A T L V
O N M T S Q R P R L O E U I
F O U A A E L E E H C C E S
T H S B O I M S T T D H C N
W P N P A O C A R A Z N C E
A L O N T Z A O G J I O A P
R L C S S E N I S U B L M X
E E U E C I V R E S S O E E
S C Y E C S T E G D A G R R
F X D A U Q S K E E G Y A O
Y Y E L L O W T A G T V S E
S R E T U P M O C I S U M R
E I V O M E D I A S T O R E
F I N O I S I V E L E T S T
S H O P P I N G D R Y E R S
```

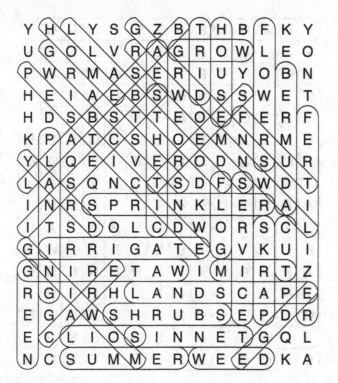

Lawns

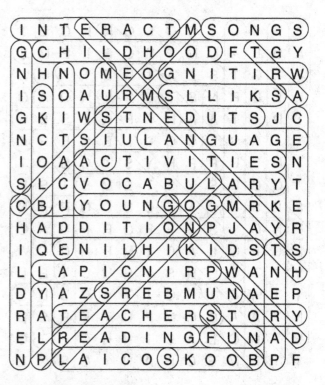

Toss a Salad

Marbles

Kindergarten

Bonsai

Sears

Engineering

Turtle Life

318

Roofs

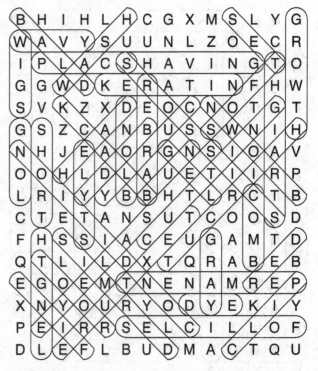

The Game of Kings

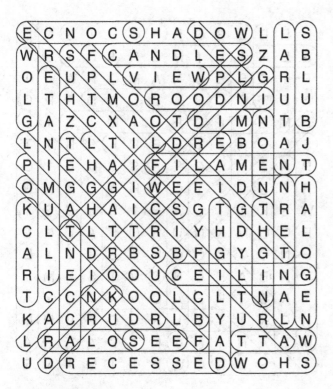

Lighting

Hair

Classic Arcade Games

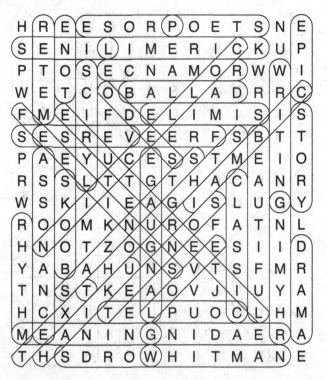

Starts with HI

Juggling

Poetic

320

Delicatessen

Digital Photography

DVD

Maize

Social Networks

Dentistry

Lock Up

History

Caffeine

Western Culture

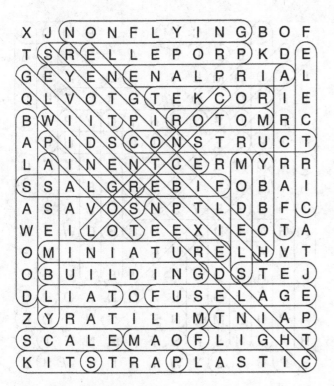

Model Aircraft

Kitchen Utensils

Trampolines

Health

Hats Off

Apartment Living

Humor Me

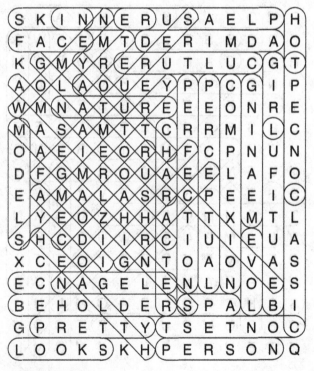

Antiques

Cable Television

Beautiful

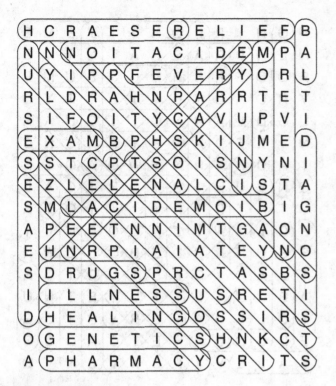

Medicine

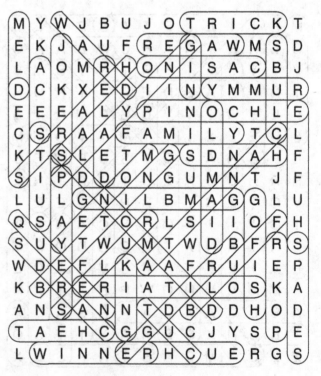

Lunar Eclipse

Pixar

Play a Card

Literary

Law

Tradesman

Exercise

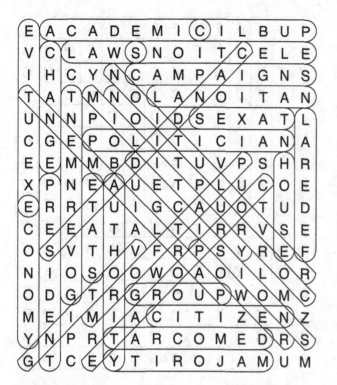

Political

Gene Study

Electronic Circuits

Iced Tea

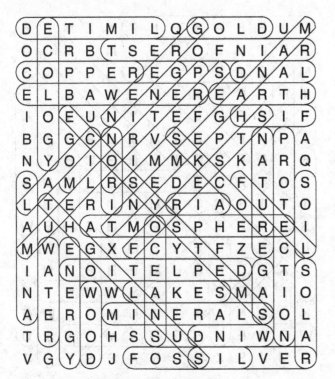

Natural Resources

Tom Hanks

Pigs

Health Provider

Rock Types

Textiles

Internet History

Paper

330

Lady Gaga

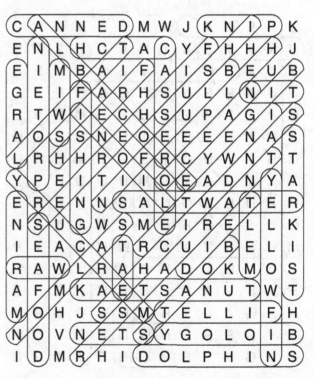

Studying Plants

Pastry

Tuna

The Lion King

Contract Bridge

Condominium

Classical Mechanics

332

Edible Seeds

Telling Time

Hewlett-Packard

Here's Some Water

Canning

The Supreme Court

Pinball

Finding Nemo

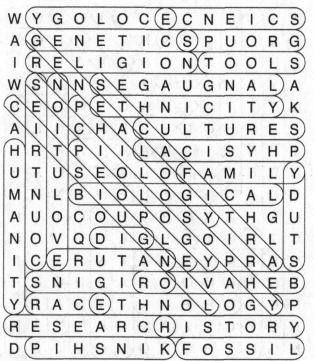

Anthropology

Benjamin Franklin

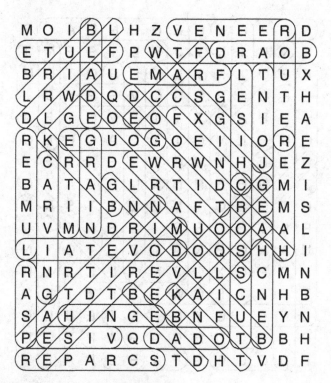

Woodworking

Coffee Varieties

Bond Movies

Fun for Kids

Model Rocket

Target Corporation

336

Going to School

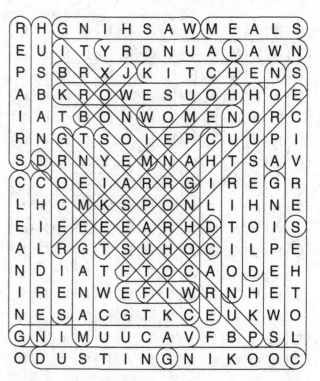

Cork

At the Library

Homemaking

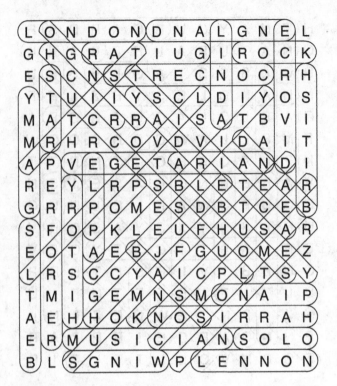

Paul McCartney

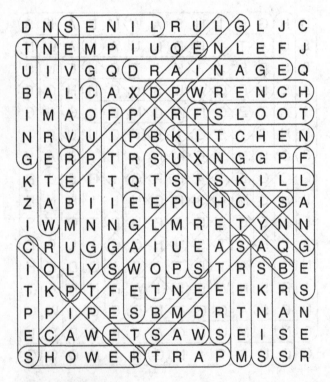

Plumbing

```
S E L L I N G N I P P O H S
P R O F I T N U O C S I D T
D U Y R E V I L E D E M B E
D E S E S A H C R U P O U L
R C P C U S T O M E R S Y T
S R M A K M O N E Y W W E U
G E A V R E L S C W H W R O
N M R Q S T C U D O R P S P
I M K V E I M M L Z H Y B R
Y O E S I T R E V D A O E I
U C T T S C S R N L U G W C
B R I O A A E S P T A K A I
L E N R L B U S I N E S S N
D G E E R I Q A S D O O G
A I R S S D U M A I L I U L
M T A C H E C K O U T K Q S
```

Retailing

```
G N I N I A R T U O K R O W
Y S E E F B A R B E L L S E
M E M B E R S H I P O O C F
N N W E L L N E S S E K I B
A I E O L G E L C S U M B T
S H I I I N S T R U C T O R
I C G D P I L A T E S F R E
U A H R T M L C O L E F A D
M M T A I M E B Q C S F M
M T S C C I B X L Y S A F M
A G O Y A W B S E C A I T
E P O O L S M N P R L I L L
T N E M P I U Q E O C L N L
S V M Y G S D L O G R I E S
A N U A S R E N I A R T S N
D M H E A L T H A C M Y S E
```

Health Club

Soft Drinks

Integrated Circuits

Professional Chef

Caterpillar

A S N T F B G C I R C U S V
B O O E O O L S P A C E C T
R C A P R N A U Z O O A I A
A I F O E O M O P S P W E T
I A R R S B I R R T M I N I
N L I A T O N O I R I L C B
S U C N C M A V M O H D E A
T V A G S O I I A N C V L H
U S G U R T M N T G O L A Y
D T N T Y E G M E L I N F E
Y R I A M N A O U R A Y A K
N E B N A M O T O N W B M N
N N M H M G I G A D I A I O
U G I A N O G B J P A T L M
F T L O N G A R M S E L Y K
Z H C R A E S E R T O O L S

Chimpanzees

S O E X P E N S I V E L Z D
W K C F G O L A N A L M T Y
I I E O O C I T I Z E N R J
S E I O I S A C P C C E A E
S S P R I N G O H H T M U W
W K E P L G C A A T R G Q E
A C M R K K N I A A O T H L
T O I E E I N B L L N E O S
C L T T C E T A D D I L U R
H C T A W P O T S I C E R I
S I L W R I S T W A T C H A
I T A S E T U N I M A A A P
L T D F A S H I O N R N E
V A E S R E B M U N W B D R
E L M L A T I G I D N A B Q
R P A R T S D N O C E S U B

Watch It

L D X E L P A M F P A P E R
V T D D E L M S U I A X Z Y
A I M S U Y R R E H C I E H
M M H M O W A G L S T O N K
M B B A F O R E S T U Y I T
K E K Y R O K C I H N O P E
R R S C E D A R D A S F H R
A T U N L A W T G L L A N Y
B D O O W T F O S O I C O L
S T R E E S H H O U G U O G
T A B L E A O R H D D T B C
A Q I O M P I S A N D W M L
I F F G G N I V R A C P A X
N I A R G N K S D R A O B S
N R U B I R C H Q B L H G F
G G R F L F M N C N S C E G

Wood

D I U Q S F G C R A B S N E
A D E E W A E S I O P R O P
S E A O T T E R S H M A M K
E E N I R A M B U S I I L R
G G U L L A A A P I R V A H
N G T I R C K B O F H A S H
O S O L T E C A T D S C N S
P N I E C T A L C R O L O M
S N R O K A B O O O Y A E O
C I R R L C P N L W S H G L
A A I G L E M E G S T W R L
L L A A P A U D I V E R U U
L E M O C N H S I F R A T S
O S D E T R I T U S S N S K
P S U L I T U A N E E L A B
S M O T A I D O L P H I N N

Marine Wildlife

340

Real Estate

Collectibles

We Have

EVERYTHING®

on Anything!

With more than 19 million copies sold, the Everything® series has become one of America's favorite resources for solving problems, learning new skills, and organizing lives. Our brand is not only recognizable—it's also welcomed.

The series is a hand-in-hand partner for people who are ready to tackle new subjects—like you!

For more information on the Everything® series, please visit *www.adamsmedia.com*.

The Everything® list spans a wide range of subjects, with more than 500 titles covering 25 different categories:

Business	History	Reference
Careers	Home Improvement	Religion
Children's Storybooks	Everything Kids	Self-Help
Computers	Languages	Sports & Fitness
Cooking	Music	Travel
Crafts and Hobbies	New Age	Wedding
Education/Schools	Parenting	Writing
Games and Puzzles	Personal Finance	
Health	Pets	